WORDS OF L♥VE TOO

WORDS OF L♥VE TOO

♥

♥

♥

♥

Penned by
Michael A. Lee

ISBN: 978-1-937449-42-1

Published by: **YAV Publications**
Asheville, North Carolina
YAV books may be purchased in bulk.
For information, please contact Books@yav.com
Visit our website: www.InterestingWriting.com
See last page for author's contact information.

1 3 5 7 9 10 8 6 4 2

Book design by A.M. Lee

Printed in the United States of America
Published February 2019

DEDICATION

To my lovely wife, Angela
Whose hand has blessed many
Especially mine. You are indeed a jewel
I Love you honey

ACKNOWLEDGEMENTS

To my dear parents
Reginald and Margaret Lee
Your love for me is a reflection of your love for God and His Kingdom

Blessings to Michelle
Our special helper, thank you

To our assigned prayer warriors
Wanda and Lindi
Along with a host of others who have interceded for us
In this and many endeavors over the years, thank you

And a huge thanks to our publisher
Chris Yavelow
Again and again through this book and volume one
Your patience, joy and insight has helped us greatly in this process

Thank you, thank you and again, thank you all

TABLE OF CONTENTS

INTRODUCTION

INTRODUCTION

Welcome to **Words of Love Too**,
the sequel to *Words of Love*,
our first collection of poems published in 2011.

As in our first volume, it is our hope and expectation for you to find that particular poem, or poems, that will speak directly to your heart and into the hearts of those that you love. This is not a collection to quickly browse through. Please take your time and slowly ponder the words before you because you may discover some poems are prophetic. And perhaps they will lead you into a deeper revelation of God's love for you.

God's love is as a house, with many timeless additions. His love never stops nor grows stagnant; it is neither a sentence that ends. Rather, it is God's never-ending story of His love for mankind. It is as a powerful rushing river, bringing life to the world.

Enjoy the journey... and enjoy the God who is Love

WORDS OF LOVE TOO

♥ ♥

SECTION ONE

THE COMMISSION
OUR MISSION

AMERICANS–AMERICANS

Americans, Americans
There are things for you to be
Americans, Americans
There are things for you to see

Prophesy the much
Prophesy the burn
Prophesy the love
Burn and be the word of God

Rock, rock, light be, love
Rain, go, love and be
Gather, gather, love and do
Love God and love this now

Commit to love and be the way
Rise miracles and be the way
Burden, burden, light, love, purpose
Commit love and love

Commit to Father and be the love
Wrestle, love and turn to Father
Rise, love, love and love
Send love, love the nation

Send love, love the nation
Rain love, burn in God
Miracle-love, light and love
So burn in love and love, American

Wrestle and be the way
Rain, love, see the day
Light, love, burn with love
Love the word and love the church

GOSPEL COMMISSION

Sign, sign, sign
Turn, burn, light love
Teach mission love
Relent! Burn with God

Red, red, abundant love
Relent, love, light
Release light, love
Release Father's light

Commission, burn love
Commission, love word
Shut in: burn love
Say and bless you see

Ember, embers, love and blend
Bless and love your marriage
Connection – it's light for you
Words burn, love you see

Connect love, light and love
Soap, soap, love, love
Release, bless, mission
Mission abundant blessing

Connect, connect
Love your marriage
Correct, love
Love be

MERRILY

Merrily, merrily, purpose is
Send love, open house
Charis, charis, God's light
Carol, carols, love and God
Reign, love, love these
Rise and love this and this
God and love and thee
Wrestle purpose and love
Light, God and love
Reign, go and love
Yeah, love, love these now
Yeah, God, light and God

LOOSED, LOOSED, LOOSED

Go and go
God sends and God sends
God sends, God sends
Separate and be
Go and go and go
Go and be and be

Learn to go, learn to have, learn to be
God learn, God learn, God learn
Learn to go, learn to have
Go and be and go

Head: you are the head
Dare it and do it
Dare it and have it
God is sending and God is sending
Ho! Go and be
You are…you be

Go! Loosed! Go! Loosed!
Learn, go and be loosed
Oh and oh and oh, tell, tell, and tell
God sends, he sends
Loosed you are, loosed you are
Learn and learn and see
Behold, it is time: go and be and do

God sends out
He sends, he sends and sends
Daddy is sending, he sends
God loosed, God loosed
Here, there…here, there
Go and do and go

Here and there you are to go
God loosed, God sends
It's time, go, God is
Ho! Go and be

God open, God blessing
Lo God is, he is
Sing, sing, and sing
God's sending, God is sending
Heed, heed and heed
Sing: God is. Sing: key in

NEIGHBOR: GOD'S LOVE

Siren, siren, siren
The word, the love, the house
God's love is for you
And God's love is for these

God's love: you're to love your neighbor
Your neighbor, your city, your church
God is on change…love now!
And God sends love

God sends grace
Release, forget, and love
And God loves your neighbor
Now fire, love fires

God's love is on your church
God's love is on your nation
God's love is on you
You're loved, you're loved

And love your neighbor
Many neighbors, many houses
It's time for you to see
Love is great, love is secret

Love is me
For God sees neighbors
God loves the neighbor
And love for you…is learning

God sees you and sees love
Light is love, and light is me
It's love for these
It's love for you

RISE

Rise, rise, love abides
Rise, rise, it releases
God's holy and blessed
Light, love, God's love

Descend, Heaven's gate
Open up, love the house
Ready, bless up!
Witches turn, see now

God's love, God's light generation
Walk and bless and love
Holler and bless the nation
Holy abiding Father

God love, God's vision
Which generation you see?
Set up, set love
Gate open, God's love

Commission – abiding love
Shuttle, shuttles, love word
Witches turn, for God's light shows
Witches, I show light

Walk and bless the house
Holy love you are
Shuttle, shuttles of Heaven
Will love, will bless the nation

Walk and worship, walk and bless
Walk and love, bless the nation
Walk and bless the nation
You bless, you see, you bless

You bless, you bless, you see
It's love of love
Its love opens honor
Love opens love

See light, mission
The blessing! The burn of God
Shoal, shoal, love God
Shoal, shoal, love of the Father

Stay open: mission, God
God mission, go see
Go live, seer see
God's love, go see

Godsend be
Be and love this, that
Will leaders love them?
You be the Father's light

LOVE IS

Opening, opening, opening now
Love is committing
Love is holy
You be love

It's love visit, seven
The love is love
Love is a visit of God
And now love is connecting now

Oh love and love oh be
Love is a beast of God
Love is the Father's mission
Oh love is God's keys

IT'S TIME TO BE

God's here
Word and love
The burn, the burn, love is
Love vision, gate, now be

Will you be and see
Walk in the Father's light
Open door, open house, love
Send love – God's light

Search and be the Father's light
Urgent grace, love and mercy
Holy love hears, mission
Surge – be the blessing of love

Heaven, sow Heaven
Love, it's time, love
Open love, open you
Open you – be light!

So abide and so abide
Enter the blessing of Heaven's light
Witches turn, love and be
Soaking grace, love and be

It's a day, it's a day, it's a day
It's shut in, it's shudders, it's love
Love is love, is love
You be, you are to see

The Father's love, the Father's blessing
The way to do is love
Send and be the blessing
And burn and love and love

It's love you be, you see
Word, word, burn love
It's love you be, you are
Gate, go, do, be

It's love you see
Open door, open love
It's love you be
Say, be and love

It's time for mission and love
It's love opens love
It's you and love and God
Shut in, worship and see

God's love you be
You be the Father's light
It's light on nation
The Father's light

The way is now
The way is now
The Father's light you be
Be and see

GOD LOVES YOU – BE

God loves, ha!
Yes! God loves you
Secret: deep is this time
Secret, secret, burn in love

It's him who is
Send, burn, light be!
Turn, do, visit, see
Build love, see how

See, be his light
See time, see
Love, time be
Send, time, time

It's love-time
See God be
Hold, love now be
See grace now, now

See time be
And be deep love
See, door, love
And be the Father's love

REALITY

This is God, it's time
This is light, see
Light see, yes
Now God see

See God deep   See light in thee
And see his gate, see? Love time be
And see light deep   Love burns, yet be
And see God   Holy time be

Deep…be deep   Hold, love and do
Shut, see, turn be   Sow and be love
God is He   And love and love this and love
Yes, He is He   It's love, it's love to be

You be this light, see Mission? Turn now
You see light be   Grace does love
See and be his light   It's God love you, see?
And love and see God   Honor Heaven's love

Love and be   See now, turn, mission
Hold and be   See light deep
Hold, see   See great time gate
See, be love   God does now

                        So do and do
                        And do, great days
                        God now does, yes
                        Hold, love mission

BE WHOLE

Pierce, pierce, see, go tears
See light, see light and see God, see
See, entering the gate
Whole, whole be, love

Whole see, whole, bless
Hands of love see
Sign, sign, sign, hearken
Do bless, see love be

Purpose, see God
Shaking, grace shaking
See, go be
Grace is light, see light

Light is Heaven's love
It's time of light
Love cycle bless now
Open Heaven's purpose, mission

Purpose is love: see and be love
Oh see my gate, tent shaking
Honor and blend in him
Holy sign be

See love, see
See God mission
Holy, see holy
It's yes, go see

FATHER'S TENTS

Healing tents of God
It's the Father now
See this nation shake
It's here, this nation
Gate, church, mission
Open the Father's light
Cycle, secret, mission, gate
It's now, the now, the day
This vision, mission, shaking
Honor and love the nation
Send words of God to this
Send and bless this nation
This share and see
See, be the Father's news
It's mission and change
See, do miracles now
Show, do, see
See the Father's gate
See and do: vision, dream
It's love vision — shake

SHOOT LOVE!

God's love…share!
God's love…grow!
Love, God's love…yes!
It's time to do…to be

It's time to be, it's time to do
The door of grace is in thee
Shut, shut, yourself in love
It's love, it's love you're to shut in grace

There's love, there's love to share and share
There's love, there's love to change and change
It's love in thee, you're to be

It's time to do: forget!
It's time to release and love
It's time to go in change
And love, love: shoot it!

LOVE IS A SOAK

Season, love and release
Leader release, secret love
Love sign, love sign
Cycle, cycle, soap, love

It's here and now
Mission secret, secret
Soak and see love's mission
It's secret, secret, secret

The love-soak, the love release
Love is soak and soak
It's love-soak, it's love
Love-soak, love you be

Living in love, secret
It's secret, it's secret, God is
Living word, it's word, it's God
It's cycle, light

SOAKING LOVE

Love is a soaking
It's love, it's soaking love
It's love, soaking love
Light, love, you soak in

It's submission, it's grace
It's God's love in thee
It's soaking, light be
Love is soaking in you

Healings, miracles, change
Heaven's love is in this
The angels of God: soaking and love
It's soakings, healings, grace

Soaking is seeing love
It's soaking, healings in thee
Love is soaking healings in you
Love is soaking you in him

Soaking, soak in love
It's love, it's you in love
It's soaking love in you
Yes, soaking, soaking you

The Father's love soaks in thee
It's love for this time
It's a sopping, sopping grace
Soap, soap, love you be

GOD IN SEVEN MERCY

Seven mercy, seven mercy
Oh the way of God is seven
The seven of God
The seven of God

Oh seven is a nation
Seven is a secret
Oh the seven of the Heaven
Is now in the seed

Seven blending, seven mercy
The seven of Heaven you are seeing now
The seven of God, the seven of mercy
Oh the seven, the seven

You're to know God is in the nations
Upper Heaven, God's love for you
A surrender of things, of things
Love is owing things

It's love, it's God, it's love
Oh the Heaven of heavens open now
The sower of Heaven is in the house
Release the seven of Heaven today

The seven – the door of Heaven
Oh seven is God's mercy
The seven of God, the seven of God
Oh the seven of Heaven for God

Commission today, commission of Heaven
Oh the seven, the seven of Heaven
The seven of God is knowing God
Abide and abide and abide: it's now

Oh grace and love and God
Angels connecting, teachings
Seven, open Heaven, mercy is God
Trust…it's mercy

Mercy, love, mystery of God
It's love, mercy and God
It's love and God and mercy
December, love is increased in grace

Upper Heaven, upper Heaven
December love, upper Heaven
It's December of God's mercy
Oh mercy, mercy, love

Real, real blessing and love
A line of God, a line of worship
A here, a now, a here, a now
Upper Heaven: send love, love, love

Mystery of God
Mystery of love
Upper Heaven, upper Heaven
Mercy, God and you

Love, love, descend, descend
Discern be, discern for God
Upper Heaven: mercy, mystery-love
It's mercy, God and you

Mercy, priests of God
It's mercy and love for you
It's seven mercy, seven mercy
The way, the word, it's mercy

LOVE'S ADVICE

Mission, God, direction
Oh love is now to be
It's time for you to know light
It's light, it's God you see
Land, land, God's light be!
Oh love goes now
So love and burn in him
Oh love and be love

It's love in me
Mission, see in me
Mission, God, you be
Love them, be now

So go, so live
Holy is this nation
Listen! See God now!
It's God, deep grace be

RECEIVE THE SEAL

Seals, seals, and seals
Dare it, dare it and receive
Love abides in love, go and love and go
Telling, telling, and telling

Telling, telling, telling
Open, open now
The pearl, the pearl, the pearl
Grow, grow, grow in my love

The goals, the goals you receive
Open, open and be and be
You're going to receive blessing
Knocking, knocking, knocking

Pearls, pearls of grace
God's love rests and rests
Direction opens and direction abides
God's, God's love blessed

TEAR IT & DARE IT

Tear it and dare it
Releasings, releasings
Goings and beings
Wrestle, wrestle, wrestle

Peril, perils, grace
Grace opens power
Blessing, blessing grace
Rooted, rooted and abundant

The doors are blessed
God and God loves the blessing
Enter the power, enter abundant
Love secrets, love blessing

Dream dreams: have dreams, release and be
It's more and more you are to see
Labor and be, labor and be
Released and go and be, released and go

HEAR, DO AND SEE

Hear and do
Hear, do and see
It's love in mission
Open door, open things

Gate of Father's love opens
You see the Father's gate
Holy cycles, yes
This new love

The love is God
Signs and love
Open house, open love
Hold, hold, love cycle

See, be the Father's light
Holy things you be
It's Heaven and light see
Holy mission do

IT'S DOOR

Things of love
This here is love
This deep door is God
It's door and Heaven

It's door, door, doors
This living love is love
It's door, it's door, it's door, it's Heaven
This door is love, you see

This living, deep Heaven
It's God of love
The love of Heaven
This God does

This day of love is now
This love of God
This word, this here, is love
Yes, time now

Your season, your knowing, your living
The will to do for love
Yes, time is God
God, do and love

LOVE'S MISSION

Here, mission, tears
Here, mission see
Tears, grace, God
Tears of love for this

Turn, missions of love
It's here you see love
See, be, light see
Dip, dip, go see

Dip in love
See love in this
It's him, it's light, it's God
Love this day you see

So turn to live
See and be his light
And be the word to this
See, be, new this

The Father goes in thee
The Father does in thee
Love is great in thee
Show his love in this

It's love, it's love, oh you see
It's love you be in this
Holy love in this
It's love in thee to be

WORDS OF LOVE TOO

♥ ♥

SECTION TWO

GOD'S CALL FOR CHANGE
CHURCH
NATIONS

THE CHANGE IS THIS

Change, change, new day
The will is God
He is here
This is Heaven

The word, the burn, the love
He abides in God
The word, the Father, the Father
This love, God of Heaven

Send love, turn things
See love deep
The will, the Father, the love
His holy time

The will, the love, the mantle
This abiding Heaven
The word is God
This love is his

This holy Heaven
This turning of Heaven
This healing God
This God does

CHEERS, CHEERS, CHEERS

The great, the great change is church
Ho, hosting: change and grace
Level, levels of change and change
The heights of grace

The heights of my love
God's rich, God's reaching, God's rich
Herod, Herod, you're not there, not here
Releasing, abide, releasing worship

Wake, wake, wakings: wake, wake
Cyber, cyber grace to be
Holy, holy, God's change
God's bring – bringing change to you

God's releasing, God's releasing
Holy, holy, God's working, working
Regenerate, regenerate, healing, healing hearts
Secret man, secret love, secret change

Herod! God's says you're not this, you're not there
Hurdles, grace, hurdles, abide
Grace, release, grace, receive
God's change, God's love, God's secret

Disciples, disciplings: change, change, change
God's regeneration: change, change, change
Rich, rich, seal, seal, seal
The work, the house, the change

Seek, seek: grace is great, is great
There's a release, there's a release
There's a work to be
Holy, holy is grace in thee

God's secrets, God's change
Drip, drip, drip, change, change? Ha-ha!
Rich, rich, shaking, shaking
Riddle, riddle, change, regenerate

Defeat, defeat? No, no, no
Host and be, host and receive
God's riddle, God's purpose
God's blending, God's a blending

DESERT CHURCH

The way is in the desert
The blessing is in a turning
The door to turning is now
Oh the door to turning is in change
Oh the blessor
The blessing is opening you to turn
The blessing, the blessing comes in change

The visitation, the visitation
God's great change
Soaking...growing love
God's word, God's love
God's love and God's seed
It's word, it's sent
It's word, work and do!

CHANGE CHURCH

Change, change church
Love what, love what you say?
Upper Heaven, love change
God loves nations, yes

Leaven, release love
Angels, release now
Upper Heaven, grace, now
Shut, shut, now lay in love

Land, land, God is love
Letter, love, love, love
Lo, love, love, nation
Upper Heaven, love, your love

Holy love, love, love
Letter, letter, lay, lay, grace, love
Shut in...see love!
Open Heaven, open house, love change

DESTINY HAS COME

Odd, odd these days
These days of love and purpose
Oh it's time for days to come
Days of great change

Oh God comes, God knows, God comes
It's time, it's now, it's day
Love, love, it's time for days to come
God's time is now, now, now

Leaven, leaven, it's now to shaken
God's turning church
God's turning a nation
It's destiny days, days, and days

THE DAY NOW IS

Time, turn, taste of love
Stand in him now
Door is, door is day
The day now is

See the day in this
Shake, shake, time, day
Light, time, turn day
Turn the nation, turn this now

Rise in the Father
Light is the Father
Love is the Father
Wonders of love in thee

See the nation turn in this
Word, God, love
Shut, shut, door now
Time enter the nation

See light time
Holy day is now
Live, time, see
What this be

See gates of hope
Holy time, love is
Waters of love this day is
Receive – burn in love

Live, time be
Senders love and be
Turn, turn things in Him
Muttering not, but love them

See the Father's day
Holy day of God
What this is, love
It's Him, the Word

The sea of Heaven enter
Oh love and be
Holy day in you
Holy time be

See God do
See light in him
Holy time of Heaven
Holy time – love

Mission do and see
Oh live time in light
Love, day, time now
Love visit, love day

Waters of Heaven
Love sees the Father
Holy day, time do
Surge, love be

Shake-up time
Time to turn
Time of God
See new day

NEXT DAYS NOW COME

Mystery, mysteries
Way, way and love
It's love, it's now time for love
It's love, it's love, it's love

Love is now for nations
It's love for your nation
It's yes, it's yes, it's yes
Love: yes, yes, yes

Upper Heaven, now secrets come
Upper Heaven, you're to know the blessing
Release and love and see
And love and love and see

Upper Heaven, upper Heaven
Love, love, love
Upper Heaven, upper Heaven
Soak in love: priests of love and God

God's love for them, prophesy love
Upper Heaven, it's love
Upper Heaven, love is love
Upper Heaven, it's love, it's God

Upper Heaven, love and love
Release and love and love
Love and love these nations
Upper Heaven, God's love for you

Priests of love and God
Upper Heaven, upper Heaven
Now nations, now come
Release and love the nation

Upper Heaven write, write and prophesy
Priests come and love
Age of God to now
Upper Heaven now come today

Upper Heaven, it's love
It's God for you
Priests and love and God
Upper Heaven, God is in thee

Release and do God's love
Priests of God, priests of the word
Priests of God, upper Heaven to come
Time to come to tents

Upper Heaven, upper Heaven, upper Heaven
Herald the way of God
Upper Heaven, upper Heaven
Now time to come

Upper Heaven, you're to see and be
It's love, it's love, it's you
Living upper Heaven: love
Upper Heaven now comes, now

Upper Heaven blessings for you
Live and love and love
Upper Heaven and God for you
Press and love and grow

Litter of God, litter of love
Blessing nations, upper Heaven love
Here and now for you to come
Oh upper Heaven come now

UPPER HEAVEN LOVE

Upper Heaven
Love is a word
Love is a house
Upper Heaven, ha, yes!

It's love, it's God, it's yes
Open Heaven, love is love
Carry love, see a nation
Open house, love is a shaking

Surrender! Love and love!
Shut in love, shut in love
Love…kind love
Shut in love and love

Kind love…God is love
God is love, God is light
Burn and love and God is light
Upper Heaven, love is love

Heal and love and love
Angels, upper Heaven grace
Upper Heaven love
Upper Heaven, God is love

It's love, it's you, it's God
Shut love in and love them
It's love, it's God, it's change
Shut in, love nation

Stir love, stir nations
Upper Heaven, kings and nations
Shut in, shut in change and love
It's love, it's God, open Heaven

Shut in, shut in, turn and change
Stay open, love nation
It's love, it's God – shut in
It's love, it's love, upper Heaven…God is

Rich, rich love
See grace in change
Shut in, love these
Burn and bless and love

Stir your heart and love
Stir your heart to love
It's God, it's love, it's God
Walk love, walk it out

It's love, walk in love
Counsel, grace, heal nations
Shut up, shut in, God is
Open Heaven: God is

Shut, shut, shut: God is love
Stirring nations, love nations
A shudder in nations now is
Open Heaven, open Heaven: God is

Urgent! Grow in love!
Surrender today to love
Shut in, love the nations
Shut in, God is light

It's God, it's love, it's love
It's love healing churches
Shut in, love nations
Shut in, God opens a nation

TIME – URGENT TIME

Shut, shut, show
Yes, it's him
Turning days
Time be here

See him in this
It's love in time
Love-time mission
You see him in light

See light, show love
Love, love, time
See love, day, time
See love-time

Time be in light
Turning the days in love
To see time enter time now
Turn time now

Light is Father's time
Love, time, time
See the Father in light
Yes, it's time to be

See this time
See light be
Live time in the Father
Time does time

Time to see these days
Yes, it's days of love
See time enter the nation
Time does turn

Time, urgent time
Light, time, turn
Light be, building up
It's the Father's day

Turning days and nation
Show the Father's day
See his time in you
Surging time, you see

Time to burn in love
Light be? Time do
Live the days of love
Yes, it's now the day

Turn days, tense seasons
Enter the daytime
Words, time, love
Senders of love

IT'S NOW, IT'S TIME

It's now, it's now
The way of love is now
It's now love and change and nation
God now...God sees

God sees and God knows
Love, the key to a nation
Love is a key to your heart
God is a need and God sees

It's love you need
It's love you know
Need you see, is grace
And God is in change and change and change

God is turning to thee
And God is opening your church to things
The word, the word
Love, love, love

God is in this day
It's now, it's now, it's time
The love, the love is in your heart
Love is in this day

It's time you know
It's time you see
Love is a time
Love is a day...love is a seed

You're loved, you're loved
And God knows, sees, sees
It's love you know, for you are to see
The way of love is God

And God sees and sees
God sees and loves
You're to know, you're to see
You're to do

God is connecting and God is showing
It's God, it's God, it's God
And God loves, he does
God is now, God is now

Love, you're to see, is God
Key, keys, love is to be
God is now connecting change
Release and love and see

You're to connect, you're to see, you're to know
Riddle, riddle: cuss? No, no
Love, it's time you do
It's time for you now, yes

Release love, open your heart
Love is now abundant now
It's love, it's you, it's God
God opens change, you are to know

Love is a love of sharing
Love is a secret of love
God loves you, and yes he is
God is love and you are loved

It's time you see, for you to know
It's time you love and love
Love is great and great and great
Love: you're to sow love to many

Repair, release, open yourself
And God loves change and love
Releasing and love and change and yes
Light, light connects change

God loves nations and change
Release, release, God loves change
God sends it, God sends it, God sends it
Release and change and change

God sends love and love
And God sends change, you're to know
Release...you're to know
Love is a connection

Connect and love your change
Love opens and love opens and love changes
God sends change, God sends blessing
And God sends you, yes, yes, yes...you

GRACE IS A SHUTTER—SEE

You, you, and yes, you
It's love for me, you see you are
You are loved, blessed and loved
It's love shaking you to grace

And love is shaking things, you see
The leaping, you see, is love
Rough you say? No, it's love
It's God, it's me, it's blessing

It's time for you to turn, to show, to release
It's time you see love in church
It's time for you to know love, in church
It's time you see grace, grace, God, and love

But God sees you – yes, he sees
It's love for a releasing church
And love, for you are to see
Many come, many see, many see

It's time for they to be in me
And see, they see the house
And say, where is grace and grace
God sees what they say

They say no to grace
For they see no grace
And God says love, love, love
The kneel, the kneelings

It's change opening now
God opens more for you
And God commands open change
Run to me, come to grace

It's grace: you know what I am
The gathering is now opening for you
Love you see is showing you
God sees you and you for this day

And do what I say
For I love you and you
It's time to come now for me
God is opening you to be

Releasing, blessing, doing
God sends you to nations
And you love, love, love
It's words, it's blessing, it's grace

God is working you in this
God works in nations, you see
God opens change
Yes, do it

It's time…abide
It's time…release
The cuss, the cussing: no, no, no
It's time to release blessing in nations

God sees you to be blessed
God opens change
God opens blessing
Love…God is God

HO, HA, HA

Ha, ha, God's nations
God's love for these you see
It's now commanding grace
And love opens change

Ha-ha, now, now, ha-ha
The way of love, ha-ha
Love, ha, ha-ha
Yes, ho-ho for this day

It's a shining love
And love shines in nation
Love commands change
The hope is commanding love

Ho-ho! Yes, yes, yes!
Love opens nations to you
Love, ho-ho! Yes, yes
God's love is yea and yes!

Ah-ha, ha-ha, yea, yea!
Oh, Yea! Command grace to be
It's now, it's change you see
Release, oh, ha-ha!
It's time for you to see

THE CUSP

Oh the cusp of hope
Oh yes, now it's time
It's time of love for you
Yes, it's time you see grace
It's time you know grace
Yes and it's time you open grace
God's love: yes, it's changing
Changing, changing you

It's now time to abide in hope
The word, the word, the cusp of love
Yes, yes, you're to open and command
Mercy loves and does
Commanding, commanding you to be
Releasing now, releasing command
God's love, riches and change
It's time for you to abide in love
And love is the key — to see

DECISIONS TO RELEASE

Release, release, God's love is now
God is God and love is God
God loves change...yes, yes
Release now, change
Release love, change, command
Release new change
Release now love

Love now and do this
It's love, it's time for you to be
Release and love and love
And God loves change
And God sends change

It's time, now see and do
Release and love and do and do
Release and love and send and send
Release and love and go and go
Love, you're to send love

Father, love, dad, love
Send, love is a love to send
Send, yes, love and love
God loves change, yes
Release and love and turn
Love, you're to love and love
It's love, it's time to send love

God is timing you to send
God is timing you to be
God is now in change, yes
It's love, it's now you're to do
Love, time, yes, now

It's love, it's love, it's yes
Release, command, command, love
And God loves, yes, yes
Release, command and bless
Release, yes, send and love

Release...changes come
Visitation grace, now love
Release, change, yes shake
It's time for this to come
Love words, love house, love, yes

Yes, come, do, see
God sends change, you see
Purge, yes...grace now
It's love, it's love, it's yes
Shoes, shoes, you see shoes
Releasing shoes to send
Visitation, healing, love, shaking

Releasing, abiding, loving, sending
God is come, he comes now
Visitation, grace, now love
Release, abide, come now
It's now to do, to be

You see, see...decide
God sees now, it's time now
It's time, it's time for you...it's time
Come, love, come, see
Send nations, send change

Release, wonders, signs, love
God sees, yes, yes
Visitation: change, you, you, yes
Rely, release, soak up, soak in
Visitate, visitation
Shut open, shut open
You see and love and send

Search, change
Search, change
Search and change
Release, send...you bless
Release: key, key, keys

Stay open, love opens
It's love, it's for you to come
Stay open, love and love
God release, godsend
Surge, surge, change, surge

Like God, like me, like love, like change
It's love you're to have
Release, command and send
Release, command: stir, stir, stir
It's love, it's God, it's yes

JUSTICE GRACE

Grace, love, grace, love
It's grace on you to do
There's grace for you, for you
And it's grace, in change for you

God's love you're to be
You're to be in nations
Going, loving, shaking
Nations, nations: change

There's change, there's love, there's God
And God loves you
And love, you're having love to be
God's love opens change

God's love answers nations
And God's love loves nations
Love, you're to be in change
Love for these who are least

The love, the love
It's my love
It's words, it's love, it's change
And love is opening nations

Love opens nations
It's love that opens change
And blessing nations to release
There's love, there's love, open Heavens

God's love opens change
Leap up! Leap up!
God's love…change!
And love opens nations

Love opens change
Operate and love in justice, justice
It's time about things
And love is: nations change!

DARK GRACE

The dark grace, the dark grace
The dark grace opens now
Doors of change, doors of grace
It's love, it's God's love for this change

There's love in this
There's love in this
There's love in this change
And God's love is in dark grace

The door is open: you're to go in
The door is open: today you're to be
God's nation, God's nation, grace, love, blessing
The door opens for this

And the door opens in change
Love, love…open change
It's God, it's grace, it's the change
And God's love is for dark grace

MOMENTS OF GRACE

The moments are now
They are moments in change
God loves now, today
And love heals you today

You love, you go, you see
Love opens things, yes you see
Love commands blessing
Love commands blessings

It's time: grace, blessing, love
The Christ loves nations
Love, love, rich, rich change
It's time, it's time for blessing – change!

Mercy commands blessing
And blessing blesses nation
The right church, no
Grace, love, blessing

Love early, love now
And love, you're to love now
Love mercy, love blessing
God loves grace and love

The blend, now the blend
Releasing mantles of grace
Loved, loved, they are loved
You are abiding in grace

Grip, grip, grip, it is grace
Grace: the purpose of grace
It's changing now you
God…change…grace

It's grace the open healing
And grace the abiding neighbor
It's time for this moment of grace
And grow, and love, and bless

It's time for you to be
God's grace you are to be
Riddle, riddle, you say where is it
It's in you, yes you

It's time for blessing
It's time you know
It's time love come
It's time for mantles

Rip, rip, rip, rip
Love is turning and bringing change
It's now for you to abide
It's living neighbors, it's grace

It's time: you know, you know what is
The anger: no, no, no
Angel, angels of grace now come
Love your neighbor, yes, yes

God is growing grace
It's grace in nations, yes
You're to be the one who sees grace
And love your neighbors for me

God's blessings open now
And God's blessings
Forget what was!
Rip, rip, this and that

You're seeing change
It's time for this
Blessing of blessing
Oh the blessing is for you

THE CANDLE

This nation now open
Oh open, open, command
This nation is a candle
This nation to come
Love opens change
Love opens change
Release, stay open to grace
It's time, it's now, command, love
God's love opens change, yes
Yes, you're to be open to love
Yet grace loves grace
God's love heals: grace
Love now, love shaking
Love blesses a nation
Love, you're to stir up in hope
And love commands now

MIGHTY CONNECTINGS

A ballot of grace
Oh the grace of change
The grace is change, yes
God's love for you is change

God, God, change, now
Get into things, get into connecting
The way is now – connect
It's word, it's word

ATTENTION

A bail, a bailing they say
Love says not this
It's now commanding, now commanding
Grace, now, change
Command, command now nations to come
The way is love to come
You're to come now, come now
Love is now to come
Love is changing – changing a nation
It's now, it's now to come for you
Love, it's now the day for you
Love is opening Heaven on you
Oh you're to see love and see
Love, the key to a nation

KEY LOVE

A way of change is change
Connecting, connecting now
God's love you're to see open nations
The way is to new change

The way, oh the way
Ho, ho, connect you
It's way great, it's now the way
Prayer, prayer, God's grace

The way abides in change
It's now a crossing in to change
God's love, God's nation, God's now
Love, love, God's love you're to have

The way of grace is change
Stay open, love, to say
Fathers now: command love
Love is the command and love is the connecting

Connect, connect, oh connect
Love, you're to be in love
The key of grace
The key is now

Yes, you're to shake: love
Shake, love, shake, love
God's love is the key
The word, the way, command you to be
Love: you're to be a change, change, change

THE SHAKERS

Oh shakers
It's these who do and be
They see, they are, they know
Love is in the shakers

The shakers
They shake, operate and do
Light they are in change
They are in change

They are in change
They are in change
It's change, oh, it's change they see
Riling, riling, they see

God sees, God sees the seeds of grace
God's shakings, God's shakers
It's time for this to come
God's shakings, yes, yes, yes

Early? It's time for this to be
The angel, the angels come
God's turn, God's change, God's news
The holy grace, the holy connections

Oh destined, oh destined for you to see
Turkey, Turkey you will see
God's shaking of you and you
The Esther, the Esthers show up now

It's now grace, love, blessing
God, God loves now
Love shakes your house and your nation
Change, change, watch your house

Release, God, is now shaking
The connecting, the connecting
It's love, love, love
God's love…change

LOVE WORK

Turn and word
Love visit, visit, shaking
Yet love is shaking this nation
Love is connecting, yes

Love is the burning mission
It's love, it's these nations
It's love, here, there, years, years
Years, love words turning nations

The word, the Father you see
The love you be
Love you are to this
The love, the Father you be

This burning love
Love, you be a love
Love you are, light mission
Oh love and burning love

Open love, commit to this
Love is God – now be
Love is light in thee
Love gets love

Oh love burns it now
The love, the love, the God
Love is love, see?
God is love

I TURN, I TRIM

The blend, the blend, I turn
The blend, yes you see nations
The blend, the blend
It's now change nations
Yes, come, change, love

The trim, I trim this and this
And God sees love, love, love
Love changes things, yes, yes, God
God changes nations
Love riddles, love commands
It's love, it's love

THE BLEND OF GOD

Dance and love
God's release
And blessing
The blend of God is love
The word of God is light
The word
The blend of love
The love of love you see
The word
The blend is love
God is love you see
God is love is love
For you

STAND UP AND BLEND

God's word: stand up and blend
It's a love, it's a hope, it's a love
It's a love blend
It's a blend, shaking nation
Blend: you're to do a blend
You're to blend
What, what, what is it?
A blend is a blend of nations

It's a blend of change
It's a blend of love
It's a blend of change
Grace, grace, grace — yes, love
You're to love, you're to sow
You're to grow
It's a blend: God's love
It's for you and you and you

It's for you to blend with me
You're to love — God's love
You're to blend, oh love, love
God's blend you're to show
It's love, it's you, it's grace
It's love, oh great blend
It's a blend of nations and nations
It's a blend of mighty and great

It's a blend for love
It's a blend for change
Love is a blend and a blend
It's a thing, it's a thing
And you're to blend: forget, forget
A blend of love, go out
It's a blend of change you're to see
You're to love

You're to be in love
Love is a blessing and a blend
And this is to be a blessing
You're to bless, you're to sow and love
It's a word, it's soaking, it's blending
Love, oh love is a blending
Greater, greater, greater
It's love, it's love, it's a blend

MISSION BLEND

Blend, blend, love God
The blend, the love of light
The light, the Father, the love
Say blend, say light, say God
Mission angel, mission love
The way of love, love
So love, so light, so God
God reign, God love

Connect, love be
Say love, say blend
Release and love the nation
Release and blend now
Release, blend and be
Release and blend to see
Release hands and love the nation
Release miracle blessings now

Commit, love, light
Release miracle blend
The mission is love
Release love now
Gate open, love God
Release sign, sign, sign
Connect, love and blend
Release mission healings

Light burn, light love
Mission, mission, God's light
Release, blend and love
Release mission light
Gate open, burn vision
Release and blend with light
Release and love the house
Commission, blessing, healing God

Gate open, mission be
Release and love the nation
Say love, say light, say God
Say love, say love, say God
Mission, mission, mission Heaven
Soak in love and God
Mission abundant blessing
So love, so bless, so know

THE BLENDS

It's the blends of grace
The blend of God
The blend, the blend
To release nations

The blend is abundance in grace
It's the blend of love and God
It's the visitation, the blend of my love
Oh the blend, the blend is love

It's love and change
It's love and grace
It's love and release
And it's love blend

It's love and God and yes!
It's love and blessing and grace
It's love and you to me

God's love
God's love: blend, blend, blend!
The blend is worship, the blend is grace
The blend is release

And the blend is my love
The blend is water
The blend is blessing
The blend is nations
The blend is change

Oh the blend: you're to be in grace
The blend is nations and nations
Oh the blend is now, the blend is you
The blend is you for me

The blend: God's love, go in and do
The blend – ho, God's love
Heal, heal, heal, the blend, the doer
Grace, grace, grace!

The blend
Oh change, worship, blessing
The blend: host it
The blend!

PAPA'S BLEND

The shutter of God
The love, the gate
Gate, love, God's love
Release! Burn love!

Proceed, love to see
Enter light: God's love
The vision, the dreams, love words
Visions entering: light, love

The blend, the vision, the Father
Vision entering generation
Direction, direction, love them
The love of God you send

Direction, blend, love see
The blend, the love of God
Up, up! Love them
The blend, the blend, God's love

See and blend
Burst, burst, bursting love
Vision, dream, light, love
This light...send this

Send the word, the love, the gate
God's love send
Shut in, release and love
Release, blend, love

Love, love season
It's love in love, in love
Sandal, sandals, light love
Release, release, burn light, love

LOVE KINGS

Kings of God; kings
Love words, kings to nations
It's love, it's the kings of nations
It's love, it's love, it's the word

Upper Heaven, the new love
Upper Heaven, it's the new love
Love, love, love, it's love, it's love, it's love
Love kings, love mystery

The way of Heaven comes now
It's love, it's love, it's God
It's love, it's God for thee
Drug, drug, love is now

Love is love for a nation
It's financed, it's grace, it's love
You are to do love
Love is love for these

It's love, it's love for these
Reckon, wrestle, wrestle; love these
Love, love, love these
Love kings, love mysteries

Love, love, the mystery of God
It's love, it's love for these
Upper Heaven, grace and love
Many, many things: loving things

It's love for these, for these
Upper Heaven, love for these
The priests, the mystery, upper Heaven – love
It's love, mercy, grace releasing many blessings

It's love, it's love, oh God is love
Oh love is in these, love is in the kings
Oh turn and turn to these nations
Higher, higher, love for these nations

Love and love and love
Love priests, God's love priests
Listen, listen for God's love
The trust of God for you
Correct, correct, but love is God

ROD LOVE

Shush, shush
Sigh, sigh
Callings of love and love
Love and love and this nation

Rod, love, God now
Shut in, love and God
Pattern, abiding love
Gather, gather, show the Father

Sod, sod; love now
Rod love, so God
Show love, show God
Gate, gate, upper Heaven

Preach God, love and this
Show love, God's seer
Guess, guess, see, see
Settle love, settle love

Telling vision – generation
Missile missing, missile missing
God will sow love and thee
Collision, love a nation

Tend, tend, God, thee
Tend, tend, you see
Rain love, burn love
Open house; love God

Rain, rain, Father's light
Rain love, rain see
Shut, love, shut, yes
Rod, rod, Father's light

Wrestle, shut and change
Pattern, writing, show love
Set and love and turn
Wrestle, see the love of love

Show love, show Father
Rod, rod, love you see
Rod love you see
Sow God, love you see

LOVE WAKES UP – RELENT

Rail, rail, rail, railing
Love is a shutting
Love is a waking
Love is a growing

God loves nations
And God loves your church
Relent, relent
And love your nation

Love your nation
It's love your nation
It's love your house
Relent – love is now

It's love, it's love, forget and love
Love, love, love and shut in love
Love your city
Love your nation

Love, it's a love word
It's time for love for you and you
Love your city
And bless your nation

God loves your nation
Bless, bless, bless this nation
Great, great, great change
It's love, it's love, it's you, and yes

God's love, God's rest
Relent, love keys
God loves nations, yes
Connect, release and do

Handle, handle, grace, love, grace
Jealous, you're to love nations
Breaking, breaking, breaking nations
Level, level, love, love

Religion? No…love nations
Love your nation
God's love
God's love for your nation

Release and love and shut yourself
Release and bless and yes and bless
Release and change and God and bless
To love, to love is God

Relent, it's now your nation
Relent, connect: love your city
Connect, release: love your church
Tense, tense, love, love

Relent, God's love heals, changes, loves
Host, host, loves' love
It's love, it's God changing nations
Level, levels of change, of nations

Career, love and bless
Receive and love nation
Love your nation, God's love is shaking
Release, love, work, work, love

Records, records of love
Love hears your nation
It's love, it's love, it's yes
It's reason, it's love, it's you

Healing, healing, healing
Subtle, subtle love is
Love is in you, you and you
And you are to love nation

Wrestle? No, God's love is growing
Relent, God's love is turning
Trestle, trestle, shaking, shakings
Shut and bless your nation

Shake, shake, shaking
Hon…hon…honor
Ho, love, love
Love, God and yes

Run, run, love
Love, grow, up
Go, love, nation
Love your nation

LOVE WAKES UP – RELENT (continued)

Awake, love nations
Release, God loves your nation
Love who and what you say
Relent, it's love nation

Relent, for it's love for your nation
Love your nation and love your seed
And love your nation today – yeah!
Command is to come, love

Can you do this you see? Yes
Surl, surl, surly nation
Holy love comes now
It's love, it's you, it's love

Holy grace, holy love
It's love, you see, it's love
Relent, love your nation
Love, love, yes, yes

Relent, you're to love nation
Relay love to your nation
It's love, it's love
It's in you: love

Release this nation
And love your nation
And love your nation
And love your nation

Shallow, shallow
God's love is to come now
Shut, shut, grow and love
And love your seed, and love your seed

SIMON, BURN WITH LOVE

Simon burn with love
Light in love in thee
Rise, bless the nation
Rise, bless this nation

Seer leaders, love and love
Enter the love of Heaven
Many things, many doors of love
Your rod, your Father is love

Descend, descend, love descend
Ready? God's love descends
Releasing light and blessing a nation
Love is light in these nations

Love is love is light
Love is light in the church
Relent! Love your nation!
Seven love, love nation

The love, the Father's love
Wonders, secrets of love
Soaking love, God's love
Enter the blessing of Heaven

Soaking is the Father's love
You're blessed, you're loved of love
Honor the Father and muster love
The love is loved of God

Descend, descend, you see the love
Rod, rod, God's love
Relent, release, love the nation
Soaking releases nation

The love, the nation, the soaker
The blessing, the blessing
You so enter the soaking
The blessing, the love of God

Secret rise, rising
The Father is love you see
Open house, love you see
Love you be, now

LOVE, LOVE, LIGHT IS

Love, love, light is
Direct light, love, God
Wrestle! God's love is here
God's light you see

Love, love, God's light
Send light to them
Light is Father's love
You're to send, you're to love

Ready, go, live, be
Ready, love...yes see
Wrestle, live, send light
You see, you are the Father's light

Vision, wrestle, the blessing
Abundance is love you see
You are, you love you see
You are, you love to see

Least, least, God's love
You see, you are to be
Vision, God's love
Ready? Go be!

God's commission, God's release
Yes blend, release and love
It's release, it's light you are
Dare to be you see

Direct love, light do
You are to love this
You see, you are to do
Gate: God's light

Descend, direction descend
You see, go out to love
You are the blend of love
You are to love

HEAR THIS NATION

Hear this nation
Endings, love, grace
Enter light, sigh, see
Oh love, love see

Say, live, see
Live, see God
See and release God
Shaking, correct shaking

Cycle, cycle, so live
See love, new day
Say and live, see
God does know

Say, see, love
Say and be love
Oh live and be love
Say, be, do

HOSTING LOVE

Simon, holy, yes love
Hosting the cycle of love
It's him, the Father's love
Here and there love is

Love is God's light
It's him, the Father
Holy this nation be
You be the love to them

THE WIND GUSTS

The wind opens today
The wind opens today
Oh the wind is now shaking you to be
The wind is great and great
The wind loves change
The wind is love and love
The wind is abiding in this day
The wind, great now, it's great
The wind, yes the wind
The wind is increasing
Answers and change
The wind, God's love opens change

The wind, oh great is this day
The wind is opening nations to grace
The wind is shaking, shaking, shaking
The wind is shaking you to turn
The wind, oh words, words, words
The wind loves, loves, loves
The wind opens nations to nations
The wind, great is this change in change
The wind, oh love, power, change
Oh the wind is changing hearts
The wind, oh you're to see, open up!
The wind, great change, change

God's wind, God's wind, it's change you see
The wind, the wind, great is it now
The wind, releasing you, releasing change
The wind, God's love, water, water
It's time for this wind to come
The wind, it's time for you to change
It's time for you to show, to show
The wind, oh change
God's love, oh it's in this wind
The wind, great is this wind
The wind, love? Yes, love
The wind is working in change

The wind, the wind
Heal, heal, heal
The wind you're to be
The wind you're to show
It's winds, it's words
It's shaking

THE PASSION OF HEAVEN

Keep keeping grace and love
The love hears, the love abides
To rest, to rest, holy is love
Walk in love, in love, in God
Washing love and love
Holy words of love
Love and love and go for God
Fathers, love, Jews and church

Holy the God is who is
Father, Heaven, Dad, God
Jew, the love of God
The stirring of God for this who sees
The Jews come for God's grace, for God's grace
The Jews love God, and bless them
Carry love and grace to these
Tap, tap into love and God

Passion, walk on God's love and God
Mission, open the nation; turn and release nations
Jews come to me
Mercy, love and see God in this
Stir nations, change is now
The knower of Heaven comes now
Cast the love and cast the God of Heaven
Time and blessing and Jews

Holy and holy for God they are
Marriage, marriage, nations, church
Preach God and bless now
Shut: Jews are connected to God
Motor, motor, holy is now
Passion for Jews now comes
Preaching, worship, blessing nations
Holy is love for nations

Here is God for shaking a nation
Holy is God in visions and change
The God of gods says prophesy nations in
Ripe, ripe they are for you
Shoe and shoes, come to God
Passion, God and you today

WORDS OF LOVE TOO

♥ ♥

SECTION THREE

WE WRESTLE
WE REND

LOVE WRESTLE

Rod, rod, light, love be
Wrestle, love, burn and love
Holy love, light and you
Word love, mercy gate

Rain-gate, light, love, God
Rod, love, light-be
Rod, light be, God is
Merry, merry God, light be

Light, light, connecting love
Rain, God love
Love, light, burn love
Holy love you see

Send, live and love
Reign and blend in love
Commit love! Love be!
Rain and love and love see

Mutter love and love the house
House and love and thee
Rain…hard rain
Rod, light be, love be

Wrestle and burn in love
Reign and burn in Father's love
So light be and love see
Rain and love and thee

So love be
Miracle, miracle, light be
Rise, miracle, light be
Rod, love and sow love

Mutter love and love
Love and love and love
Light be, light see
Rain, light be

Rise, rise, light be, rise
Holy love, so light be!
Merry gate, love burn
Reign, light be, go love, see

Merrily go, show God's light
Reign and love the Father
So love and go and be
Rain and love to see

So love and love see
So light be and light see
Rain and light be
Turn, light be, so love be

LOVE WRESTLE – Part II

Ha, ha, yea, see
Rain and God and thee
Rise, light and love
Wrestle, light be, Heaven's light

Rain, light, light be
Rain, light, light see
Surrender, love and gate open, see
Rain and love and God

Release and love and turn, wrestle mystery
Miracle light and love
Rain, open house, light be
Light be, God is, light be

Receive and light be, see
Light be and release, miracle be
Light, light, God's love
Tell love and love this

To release, to love, to love
Mystery: love and God
Wrestle, go and love
Light and love and love

JACOB'S TREK

Stand and love
Send, rend, God
God and love and send
Rend: it's love, it's light for you

Wrestle, love and love
Walk the gate, walk the love
Send light, send grace, love
It's light for you, you see

Rend, rend, God's wrestling
Ready, go, live, see
Word love, direction gate
God's love see, love release

God's send, God's love, God's light
God is light for you
Wind, light, winds of God
Wind of love you see

Great angel, wrestling, light
Will love, release light
God's entering – love new
God is love you see

Wrestle, burn with love
Word of God, love you see
God, love you see
Word, love, God, love

You see, go see
You see, go see
You see and be
God is love to stay

Miracle grace, say and be
Oh love you see is light
Wrestle, love is light
God is love, yes

Open, love and live
Open and love you see
Open, love is light
God is love you see

Love is light for you
Rend, light, rend, love
Light and love vision
Wrestle and live – forget

Get and love
Love for you is love
You see, you see, God love
Wrestle, you see, is light

Regenerate and love
Word love, God love
Open visions, open God
God is love for you

The word, the secret, the gate
Light is Father's love
Rend, love, go live
Wrestle, you burn with love

Love goes and loves
It's you and love for God
Rending and love is love
Is love, is love you are

God is love
Sandal, sandal, God you see
God love you see
Love opens love

Open, do and be
Rend and see
Oh live and love you see
Rend for God's love

You see, you be the love
Rend and love you see
Wrestle and love to this, to this
Rend, burn and love

God's ready, God's wrestle
You are, you are the vision
Wrestle love and God
Wrestle, for blessing is now

JACOB'S TREK (continued)

Wrestle and wrestle and be
Get in the deep of love
Be and be the be
Rend, rend, love is love

It's love you are
You are to be
It's love to see
It's love you are

Judah love, Judah live
Wrestle, live and love
God's land, God's sand
God's love, love you

It's shutter, it's love, it's God
It's wrestle, it's grace, it's light
Mission: get and love
Get and love

WRESTLE & HOBBLE

Hobble, hobble
Wrestle and hear
Wrestle many days
Wrestle, miracles enter

To release, to see, to see
Miracle, miracle, healing gate
Major hand, God's light
Sowing miracle light

Wells, Heaven, light, you
Heaven, miracle-love
Word, light, God's light
Miracle light you see

Wrestle, wrestle
Has…has...hassle
Wrestle, love and gate open
Burden, burden, light be!

Oh perceive, release and be
Open house, mutter love is
Wrestle, love and go do
Wrestle and love in thee

Walk and love and be
Mutter love and love
Love honors Heaven
Wrestle, mutter, light be
Commit! Light be!

WRESTLING LOVE

Reckon Heaven, reckon light
Wrestle, light is love
Light, love, Heaven's light
Wrestle, wrestle, light be!

Commit and light and love
Live and love and be
Rise and love and do
Rise and do the word of love

Collision, collision
Love, love, be
Rise, burn with love and see
Rest, rest, love, be me

Gate, go, love this
Rise and love this now
Rise and love this love
Rise, perch, rise, perch

Kairos, kairos, light and love
Miracle love and Heaven
Rise, love, love you
Wrestle, bless, connect and live

Rain, rain God's love
Rise with vision and love
God and love you see
Rise and be the word to see

Major miracle, love and this
Commit, burn with love for this
Nestle, wrestle, burn and light be
Oh burn with love for this you see

Wrestle! Light and love
Wrestle! Light and love
Show love and day, day, day
Rain love, rain you see

Rain, you see light and love
Rain and love on this you know
Rise, open and live in this
Gate, go and love this

Love, love this and this
Rain God's light you see
Purpose, miracles, love and thee
Rise, purpose, light, love

Wrestle, go, stay love
Wrestle, connect and love the Word
Wrestle, miracle, miracle, miracle
Wrestle, connect and live the word

WRESTLE, MIRACLE-LOVE

Much miracle, much God
Hold, love, hold, love
Wrestle! Light be, miracle-love
Wrestle, light be! Light be!

Major light, light, love
Wrestle, love and love
Wrestle and love and love
Wrestle and blend and love

Press and bless and get now
Wrestle, shoo! Love be!
Wrestle, gate open, do be
Wrestle, light be, love be, see

Miracle gate, love word, see
Miracle gate, light be
Wrestle, answers, light be
Missile gate, release God's light
Wrestle, miracle-love

SEND, DESCEND

Send, descend
The secret, the secret
The secret of miracles is light
Wrestle, love and see

The seer, the secret, the secret
The secret, the vision, the secret
Send, send, send
Send the light, send the secret

Wrestle, teach, wrestle
Commit and love and see
To wrestle, to love, to see
The seas, the seas: light and love

LOVE WRESTLE – Part III

The will of God
Wrestle, love and blend in love
Ah, wah-la-la
Ah-rah, la-la

Light, love, God, love
Love, light, burn love
Rain, light, God's love
Light, love, God, yes

Miracle, love and love
Light, love and love
Rod, love, God's light
Rod, love, God's light

Sow miracles, love and love
Wrestle and love and be
Purpose light, burn and love
Gate, light, burn and be

God, God, love you
Wrestling, burn, loving thee
Wrestle, burn, love this and this
Consent, love and do

Rain, miracle-love
Rain, love thee
Purse, purse, God's light
Right, right, light and love

Rain purpose, rain Heaven
Rain, miracle-love
God love, God right
Rise, love, light and love

Wrestle, light and God
Rise, light, rise light
Person love, person love
Wrestling…miracle-love

Commit love and love
Rise and receive the love
Gate, light, upper Heaven
Wrestling, wrestling – you are a blessing

God and love and you
Piercing, piercing, love you
Reign, go, light and love
Rise, light, love yea!

Wrestle, wrestle
God and this
Rain, miracle-love
Wrestling, wrestling miracle-love

REND THE GATE

It's gate open
777
Ready, ready, ready
God is
Shut, shut, this is a shut
Rend, rend
Gate now
Rend now
Rend that
So, so, light be!
This, that great grace now is
Wrestle, wrestle
Gate now see
So blend
So see
Light be
God see
Oh see and see
Light be!

RENDING

Show, shows
Shutter, shutters
Rend, rend, you see
The word is, gate shut

Rending, greater grace
Rending is grace and love
Rend, light, rend, God
Gate release and burn love

TAG TEAM

Purpose, gate, God and thee
Miracle and love and God
Heaven, light, God and thee
Major gate, Heaven and thee

Miracle light, Heaven's love
Wrestle and light be for you
Fast, love, love-gate open
Shut, shut, shudders of Heaven

Rain and love and you
Wrestle, wrestle, you see the gate
Miracle, miracle, love and thee
Shuttle, shuttles, light of God

Soak, light and love
Wrestle and go and love
Wrestle and love and you
Sow and love and sow the light

Wrestle and wrestle, gate and light be
Wrestle and love and see
Wrestle, purpose, Heaven's Heaven
Sow and love and love

Light be! Gate now see
Rain, major miracle, Heaven
Wrestle, love and go
Passion, love and God

Miracle, go and do
Holy and love and love
Wrestle and love and light be
Father God, love, yes

You're to love, you're to love
You're to sow God's love
Wrestle and be the word
Soak light and show light

American gate – light be
Rain and love for this day
Rain and light be, see, nation
Rain to light, to light

Love and love and gate open
Rain and love and thee
God and thee you see
God and thee you see

Miracle, miracle, God and thee
Miracle love and God you see
Wah-wah, God's light is in thee
Wrestle! It's time, it's love, it's nation

Soap, soap, love and blend
Wrestle, go and love
Wrestle, miracle, Heaven's now
Wrestle, wrestle, send the word

It's love, it's God you are to see
A 'burd', a burden of Heaven
Rain, light, you are, be
Gust, gust, love word

Descend, descend: the word is Heaven
The mercy, the gate, the vision
Rise and love and love
Love is love you see

Rain, miracles, light be
Wah-wah love and love
Love, love, you see, the love
Rain, light and God you sow

Rain, rain do you sow
Rain, rain do you send
Light, love, holy love
Pattern: love and thee

DIVINE PURPOSE

It is the purpose
It is the purpose
Endings and release
Watch the gate and love the nation

Enter the gate and love the nation
Enter the secret: light is love
Wrestle and release, burns and burns
Rend, rend, God's release

Men, many things release
Rend, rend, God's light
Rend and burn love's light
Open door, light release

Miracle grace, God's love
Marriages, grace, grow love
Commission, release and burn
The seer, the light, the secret

Open secret, open grace, open love
Rend and be the secret
The burn, the gate, the secret
Rend with love, with love, with light

WORDS OF LOVE TOO

♥ ♥

SECTION FOUR

RAINING WORD

RAIN GOD RAIN

Well, well
Great gate open now
Live shut, live love
Rain, God, rain

Rain, love rain
Rain, live, love
See love, love now
Rain, God, rain

To see, to see
It's God in thee
Rain, rain, God's rain
Well, wells, word, love
So love, show light

RAIN OPEN HOUSE

Shush up
Shut, shut now, shut in
Rod, burn and turn
Rod, love and be

Joel, Joel, Joel, Joel
Mercy gate of God
Rod, love now
Rod, open now

Rain, love and be
Rain and love and change
Rain, open house, rain
Open house, open house – do it!

Open house, open house, open light
Rain, light and change
Rod and God and you
Rod and you and love

Release love, open love, see it
Open house, open love
Love abundant, love abundant
Rain and love and love

Rain and you and love
Love...open love
Rod, burn, shoo-shoo
Rod, open, God

Rod, go and love
Rod, love nation
Love, love and thee
It's love, it's you, it's least

Rain gate, open house
Abide and love and see
Open house, open house see
Rod, open house, be

Press, burn and love
Open aide, open house
Rod, love and thee
Seven, love thee

Seven, love ye
Rain, least, love
Love and love and love
Love and light and shut in

Rain, God and shoo and shoo
Sow and love and shut
Oh love, show out
Wrestle, open here now

Seven, open up
Rain gate of Heaven
Open house, open house, leader be
Set love, set change, set yeah!

Rod, love you
Release, burn and love
Light, live and show
Seven, open Heaven

Open house, open love
Love and love and love
Oh love opens houses

SEE A NEW DAY

Tears, new day
It's time for grace to be
It's love, see?
See love now
See his grace in you
See his word be
See his word be
Holy be

Oh see and see this love in this
See his word you see
Oh see the Father now
Say blessing and love
Oh say and be
Love see, be
It's love, it's love be
Say, bless and be

HEAVEN IS OPEN NOW

Heaven is open now
The watcher, the Father
The watch, the gate
Know it's love

The word, the know, the gate
The secret, the gate, the know
The dew of Heaven know
The house of God the Father

A burning angel opens Heaven
It's Heaven, directions and know
A burn, a gate, a God
The word of God: love

The watch know, the door is
The word, the dew is
A burn, a door, a hope
The word, the door know

This watch is Heaven
The gate, the Heaven, the know
The word, the Heaven see
The house, the gate know
This house know

THE PRAYER WAY

In search, it's a search
Here, there, where
Where, there... where, there
The way, the way is prayer

Ho and ho it is there
Lo, lo and lo, the way is prayer
Learn and learn: it's the way
Learn to go and go and go

Leper, leper, leper
God is in this thing
He is on this way
Wish is a word

Prayer is a thing
Ho, ho, ho, it's a thing
Ho heal!
Ho! Heal!

God's on the word
God's on this word
It's the word, it's the way
It's prayer

It's the word!
It's the word!
It's the word!
God is in this thing

The word, the blessing
God and God and the word
The word is the way
God and blessing and God and grace

THE PRESS

God says, the press
The press: no, no, no
The press: no, no, no
God's knowing, God's press

The word, the word
Nations now come
The word, the word
Change is come
The way is love
The way is commanding grace

Daddy, daddy comes now
The word, the word shaking now
It's now, the nations, nations
Nations, God's nations

The word, the word, the word is love
It's love visiting nations
Love commands change
Love opens you to nations
Love, oh love is a word for you
The candor you say? Oh no, no

Grace is in change now
Love releases blessings on you
You're to stir
You're to say love, love, grace

Stop the press, stop the presses!
It's love, it's grace
It's secrets opening for nations
Oh release the word, release grace
Operate the way of love
Doors: love, love, love

The cussing you say, the cussing
It's love, it's nations, it's grace
The rod of love is opening on nations
There's love on nations, you see

It's love, hope, grace
Love, forget what you see!
Love commands change
The way is change, but love

Releasing, releasing love, blessing, love
God's love for your nation
God's love for your church
The word, the word
Is blessing, blessing – change
It's love for the press

Love for the church
Love for the nation
God's word is the word
The word, the word…the press

WAITING and WAITING

Waiting and waiting
Words and love
What is the word?
Love is

Love key, love here
Love here, love more, love in
Lift, light, lift the light
The palace is great and the palace is open

What dues, what dues you say?
Holy is this thing
Holy is the word
There is a blessed, there's a blessed

Waiting, waiting
It's dad's door
It opens here
Surge and bless, surge and bless

Waiting, waiting, waiting
Word is the key
Word is to be
Word and word

THIS IS A SHILL

This is a shill
And this is a seed
Oh the seed and the word
The hassle, the hassle, the hassle

This is a thing, oh the word
Westward, the word
Westward the word
It's a word, the word

Where, where this is, where, where this is
Where the word is, is in thee
The word you're to be
Learn and be

Ho and ho, you are to see
Learn to hide it to thee
Holy is this visitation
It's a holy thing

Lesser, lesser you say
Ho, ho, ho! This is my blessing
God is open, God is tuning
God is open, he is turning

God, God, God is going, he's coming
Laban, abased, he is abased
God answers in grace
Attested, but blessed

Hobble, hobble, hobble
Lesson, lesson abiding
Hope is open, hope is great
Say, say, oh the blessing is opening this day!

Sermon, sermon
But oh I AM
God is in thee
Oh, but he is in thee

Learn and be and receive
The least, God is in
The face, the face is they in me
Hope in me, God is in thee

Courage you are in me
Courage, you are to be
Oh see, oh see, oh see
You are to know it's to be

It's to be, it's to be, it's to be
It's to be and you are to be
Hopes, hopes, hopes
God is in this

Bell, bell, bell and bell
God is in this day
Oh God is in this day
He is in this day

Add, add and add you are to do
Here and there you are to see
Blessed, and blessed and blessed this is
Tested and you are loved

Hedge, hedge, hedge
I stir the hedge
Abased, God is great
Abased, I AM abundant

Watch the word
Watch the word
I AM
The Word

Temple, temple, temples
Get open, get open, get open!
The amazed, I am calling this door
Fill, fill, and fill this place

The ends, the ends, the ends
Roman gods?
But I AM
The wrestle

The wrestle
The wrestle
God is this
He is the one

SEE LOVE-TIME

See love-time
Abiding love-day
Open doors of Heaven
This love is

Love, love, love
It's Heaven's here
You are abiding in it
So love, yes

Love is loving love
It's Heaven's holy love
See love deep
Love is secrets of Heaven

Secrets of God
Holy love see
Holy secrets of Heaven
So hold and love

See the Father's gate
The word, the burn
The love of love
God is here

The love is light
See light in this
God turns days
Turning days now

Stay love, stay in
Secret day of love
Stay love in love
Door of love see

This light is this day
See His word in love
Love, live, be
Love, yes, see

The word, the dew is
Love time, time
So holy this, see
Live burning in love

See the word of Heaven
This is God
The word, the burn, the nation
It's this, yes

This light of love
So abide this day
Say, say, say
Love, live love

Secret of Heaven
The love is of God
The word, the burn of God
So holy love

So loving love
The love of God
God does, you love
Yes God is love

Secret turnings of love
Sow it, sow love
Love is words of God
The Father is secret in you

So love, you
So live in Him
Show the love of Heaven
See in love

UPPER HEAVENS COME

Up, up, God is love
Love, love, nations in God
Up, and God, and yes
Heaven sees a nation

Upper Heavens come to you
Upper Heavens open now
Love is on nations now
It's love, it's God and you

It's God visiting you
It's you and thee for God
Here and God and now
Upper Heavens, you're seeing God

Upper Heavens here and now
Upper Heavens now for God
Now God is here and there
It's love, God is you

Here and you and love
It's love, it's God, you are
It's you and love for God
It's you and God in secret

Upper Heavens, changing you
Love and love you
Here and there and you
Oh love and you, love

Upper Heavens, love and love
Here is God and you are in love
Upper Heavens you are to abide in
Upper Heavens niche, niche

Upper, upper, hope and love
Hosting utter love
It's you for God, and yes you
Release God's love: yes, yes

Upper Heavens, yet God's love comes
Hosting upper Heavens, love you
Open Heavens, open Heavens come and love
Upper Heavens, oh love comes and loves

Abide, come and be in God
Up, up, love nation
Here and now God is in you
Oh love and love, yes you

Utter love, hosting love
Cuss...no love
Love is God and love is you in God
It's love, it's you and you

Leader, leader, love these nations
Wrestle, open God's love
Upper Heavens, cuss? Love and love
It's God loving these nations

Upper Heavens you see love
Upper Heavens, upper Heavens here and now
Upper Heavens, know God is
Oh love operates in God

Abide, cuss no, love
Upper Heavens, upper Heavens: you see love
Upper Heavens, now God is
Upper Heavens, do you know?

Oh love is God and you
Upper Heavens, oh upper Heavens
Oh releasing love for you and they
Urging love and God

Odors of God: love
Angels are increasing love
Hosting God in love, open Heavens
Upper Heavens, God is here

Operate in love, it's God for you
Oh love, oh love your secret love
A surrender, a surrender, a surrender
Upper Heavens, yes, you

God is soaking nations
Upper Heavens, soaking nations
Love and love and love
Upper Heavens, seeking God, seek God

WORDS OF LOVE TOO

♥ ♥

SECTION FIVE

BURNING & LEARNING

GOD'S EMBERS

Set, set, God's love
Upper Heaven, love you see
Shut, shudders, love, love
You are, you be the Father's light

Wrestle, abide in the word
Embers of light in love
Ember, embers, God's light for you
Gate, love, say God
Discern and love and love
Releasing angels now
Releasing embers of love
The Father is abiding

God's light is yes
Yes, light, light you see
The gate, the Father, the blessing
Releasing love and burning love
The blessing, the God who is
You are the blessing of love
Relent and love
Oh loving love you are

You are love on this
Open now, go see
Mercy, love, light
Releasing and burning in love
The way is light
Go out and see
Release love on things you see
God's light you are

God's burn, God's light
You are a burning light
You be and be the light
You be, see and love
God's abundant light
Releasing miracle light
Embers and love light
You are light, God's light
Day love, gate light
Love, love, see love
You see, you be love
Gate love, burn light

The Father is light
You are love you see
You are, you be
You see, you be

You are to see
Release embers of love
You are, you be love
Embers, you are love
God's embers you are
You be and see
Embers of love and love
Releasing embers of light

Answer light!
Relenting and loving now
You are blending love
Oh lovings, lovings and love
Releasing love miracle
Yes, honor love
Gates, embers, neighbors
Yes, you are light

God's love
Releasing abundant light
You are light
Get and love
God's light
You be love and light
The man, the love, you are
Ember love

Marriage: God's light
Say and love
Open door, love and be
You are a light you see
You see, light and light
Ember, embers: love light
You are love and love
Release love, it's love you see
God's love you be
Relent and love your marriage
God's love, God's light you are
You are lovings, lovings, loving

EMBER LOVE

Commit to love
Ember love, light see
Yes, burn, love see
Letter, letter, love words

It's light, it's love you see
God's light you see
It's light, go love
God's light: you love

God's love you see
Gate open, burn love
God's light, go love
God's love, God's light you are

You're blessed, you love, go do
God's love, go, see
Love, love, God's light see?
Ready, go, love light

Gate open, go see
Release, burn with love
Release and love this and this
Wrestle, go love now

Release and love you are
Yea light…love, God's love
Release and bless, you be
Gate release, bless and be

God's light: go, bless, see
Release and bless, you are
You are, you are, you are
You are, you are, you are

Release, blessed you are
God's love you be
Open, love light
Ember, love, love

God, send blessing
You are the love
Love is light – go see, God's light be
God's love, God's blessed, God's sea

Embers, go, blending see
You be, you are to see
God's light stirring up
It's love, go see

You're ready, you're loved, you're loved
Embers, love is love
You see, you are to be
God's light…burning love

BURNING EMBERS

Set, set light
Age's love light
Wrestle, love is light
Say love, love you see

Answer love with love
Send light to this you know
Love is love for gates of God
Embers, burning love
Great angel, great love
Abide, love, open love
Release and love
Forget now

It's love, go love
Member, members love
Embers burning, burning now
End now, be light

God's love, burn love
Great love, God's light
Release miracle love
Abundant blessing, love you see
Gate open, connect love
Ember burn, burn, light see
Love loves light
Embers enter, blessing love

MYSTERY

Mystery, prophesy
To shut, to shut
And light is entering you
Judah, rod and God

Heaven, Heaven, purpose Heaven
Miracle, miracle
God love see
To lay, to lay, to love, to say

Rain, burn light and thee
Rise, be light in this day
Release and burn with God in this day
Raising mystery, see? Shutter, shutter

To wrestle, to shut, to do
Correct, connect and do
Miracle, miracle, light be
Rise, light be – God is!

Creature, purpose, abide in God
Rise, blend and be
Receive, burn and love
Receive and burn with love and God

Shut, shut, shutter: light be
To love, to change, to rise
Burden light, God and change
Preacher, prophet, light and purpose

LOVE'S BURNING LIGHT

Shut, shut what is
The thing, the way is light
Light be, see me
Release mission light
Release the blessing in mission
Share light…love hard
Perceive love in hands
Say light be and love these

Shudder release, shudder embers
Embers, healing grace
Release and bless the nation
Releasing healing, healing
Say love, heal now
Say light and be Father's light
Say light, light and be
Release and bless the nation

Shudder, shudder, shudder
Release the blessing and bless the nation
The word, the blessing you are
God is light: burn, love, shut in
God is light, God is love, see love
Say love and blessing is
Here, there, the word, the blessing
The word, the secret

The light you are
The word, the nation, God's light
The way is love today
The way is love is…say
The word, the blessing you're to sow
The way is gate of God
The Father, the blend of love
The word, the Father you see

God and thee, see
You be, you are, you see
Say and love today
Release and burn with me
The word, the sea, the blessing
Embers, holy abundance
Embers, healing light
Say blessing, light you are

THE FATHER'S LIGHTS

Words, go and be
See, be love
See and love you are
You see, you be love

Seated, seated love
Embers of God in love
Embers of love you are
Embers of God you be

You be, you see
Wrestle and be the Father's light
The light of God you are
Light burns, but light is

Yes, it is
The Father's light
The Father's light of love
The Father's love you are

You be, you are to be
See the Father's light
You be, you be the Father's light
You be what God's light is

Descend, descend, light now
You be light in house
Oh blessing and love you be
God's light be

Gate open, turn
The Father's love
Embers, embers, the Father's light
You be, you are to see

You are to see
Get out, see and be
The Father's abundant light
Commit, shut in love

The vision, the vision of God
Embers and love words
You be love, you be light
Gate open, see and love

The blessing is God
Gate opens, gate release
Releasing abundant light
Releasing light, forgetting

Embers... releasing love
Releasing the Father's light
Releasing embers of love
God's light you be

You say, you say, you are
Releasing in love the fathers
Releasing, you are a father
Releasing and love

Releasing and love
God's light you be
You be, you love, you see
God's love you see

The word of God
Discern the love in me
Release and love the nation
Open house, light is God

Release the words of love
Merrily bless and love
Embers, words and light
Urgent love you be

You be Father's love
Gate be, see
Say and love and be
You see the love in these

The word, the Father's blessing
Say and bless and see
Descend, descend, be a light
Releasing love to deep light

LEARN TO LOVE

The waking, the waking, connection
The word, change and change
It's change, it's love, it's turning
The way is to turn and turn

The way is working, the way is doing
Learn about grace and love
Learn to do, love and be
And be the word and be stirred up

Love is a shaking, it's a stirring
Love is learning to do
And love is stirring your heart to change
Love will turn nations, yes!

God stirs and stirs a nation
To release is to turn
To release is to see
God's shaking, God's leading, God's shaking

Learn and see and learn
See, see, and learn to be
See, and love, and learn
Learn, learn, stay in love

And love opens change
Abide, abide, connect, connect
Bring the way and see the nation
And bless, bless and love

God's love is a secret change
And love blesses your love
Blessor blessing, God connects
God shows blessing change

This is connecting, this is connecting
The word, the word, yes, you
The word stirs you, yes you
It's love, it's love, it's connecting

Love...stay in it

TURN AND LEARN AND BE

God learnt, God learnt
You're to be and go
The word, the visitation
Visitation going and going

Let, let and let God
Learn in God, learn in him
Here the word, there is the word
Here and there you are to do

Learn: God is doing
Learn: God is being
Defy this, defy that
Oh it's grace, it's grace

God is in this hope
Ho and go and be
Level, level it's now
It's today, it's today, it's today

The old are the ones to be
They are the ones who are blessed
The blessed, the blessed: the ones they are
God sends them, oh they are the ones

Who are they?
The ones who are the ones
God is in the ones
God is on these, God is on them

BE THE FATHER'S LIGHT

Mighty, mighty, here, there
The Father's turning a nation
Love's entering your house to be
Mission: enter the Father

The Father's connecting and releasing
He is the vision
And love is connecting, connecting, healing
Love is mission to be

Oh burn and be with love
The Father be to be
Oh burning up, burning out, be the father
The father you be

You burn and love
You burn and be the Father's light
In love burnings be the Father's love
Love is the burning of miracle

Light be, light is
Light be, light see
Oh blend and love, the open house be
Light is, light be

WORDS OF LOVE TOO

♥ ♥

SECTION SIX

MARRIAGES

MARRIAGE, GOD AND LOVE

Marriage, God and love
Live, bless and grow
Live and blend and light be
Sow love and Heaven's blessing

Love, light and Heaven
Light be, light see
Love holds love
Light be…ah, light be

Light be, ah, light be
Ah love, burn and love
Oh light, love light
Say light, love and be

Oh love, burn with love
Oh live and love this
Sow love and burn with love
Love is God this day

Sow love and light and God
God and yes, God
Light is love and Heaven's abundance
Love and love, oh go be

BREAK HEART

Break heart, break heart
Way God love
Love earned? No
Love yes? Love, love

Love breaks the heart
Love heals
Love heart, love heart, love heart
Love, the key to these

It's to learn, it's to receive
It's to receive, it's to lead
Love is a key
Love is me

THE HOUSE OF SEVEN LOVES

The house
The season of light
Show love and God
Rise, light and love

Wrestle: God and thee
Wrestle: purpose and thee
Proceed, proceed: release and love
Receive the blessing of light

Soap, soap, blessing love
Purpose, visit, see the house
Rise, live, sow love
Correct, correct, abide and be

Proceed, proceed to love, to be
Light, love and love-shoes
Send destiny light
Wrestle, commit and blend in

Seven abide, love is love
Rain light, light gate
Connect light and love
Commit and love God

Sowing love and love
Commit and love your marriage
Show love and love in thee
Correct! The Father is love

Seven, seven, the Father is light
Process, love is a purpose
Show love, open house love
Shut in: love, love and deep light

Seven, God, seven
Rise, be the light of God
Rest, rest, light of love
Show the Father to this, to that

Rising commissions, rise and love
Rise to God and be the way
Sowing, burn and love
Wrestle, mystery and purpose

THE SHACKLE

The blind, the shackle
The word, the blessing
The blessor opens things
Love opens change

Labor rocking, labor rocking
Desolate change…but great change
Daddy loves abundant grace
Blessor, blessor, ho-ho, grace

Daddy loves, daddy changing, daddy shaking
Living, living, love, love and love
God and grace
God loves, love, loves thee

Dad, dad loves change
Hurdles, hurdles
But grace, secrets shaking
God shaking, shaking, shaking

Regenerate, regenerate
The blessing change, shaking
Leaders: change, change and change
The love, the blessing, the turning

The riddle, the blessing, the heart
Dabble, dabble, dabble
Hold, holding love
God loves love

The blind see and do and see
The blessing opens you to see
Livings, learnings, secrets
This gold, this change, this love

Tender grace, tender change
Love learns and grows
God's love hurts and grows
Heal, heals, change, change

Huddle in me, huddle to be
God's love blending you and thee
Riddle, riddle, change, blending
Forget: change, love, sing

God and love today, see
Love: be, be, be and be and see
Release and release and sing
The right, the right is blessing change

Bless, love, bless, heal
Abased blessors, holding grace
Higher, higher, love, love
The bride, the bride

Grace, grace
Destined love, destined change
Fighting, fighting
Love is abiding

Bail, bails, change and change
God is in change and change
Riddle, riddle, losing
The finance, the change

Release and release
Learn and see
Height, height – grace is me
Abide love, abide release

Healing, healing, shaking, shaking
Ascend and ascend
You're to release, release
The rich abased, the rich abased

Late, late, change, change
Grace, grace, love blinding
The wake, the wake
Change loves blessing

Height, height, least, least
God's love, God's love, change, love
God is in the house
Is God, is God, is God

GOD IS LOVE

Love in love, love in God
Here is love – God
Here love is – God
Love God is – yes

God is now, love
Love is God, love
Love God more
Oh God's singing love

Oh holy, and God is
Living in love, so love
Here, oh here turn
Love turn now

Oh love and turn
So love and turn
Love is, turn now
New, love, new, God

Oh love, oh live, oh do
Do be now
Holy is God, love
Burn now in Him

See it, do it, and live
Love turn, generate it
Oh tent of love, do it
Holy is, new light be!

God is God now
Oh gate open, see
It's living love here now
Love now do

BARREN BUT BLESSED

Tent, tent and tent
God opens things
Oh great tent, great tent
Oh the tent is open

Oh love is going to change
Oh lay and pray and pray
Who loves, who loves?
Word loves, word loves

Where, where is your tent?
Where is the tent?
The key is bless, the key is bless
The word is seed

It's work, it's work they say
Barren they say, it's barren
But blessed I say, you're blessed
Blessed of my love

Love is a letter of the blessor
Love is a leader who blesses
Love is a tent that increases
Word loves, word blending, word blesses

THIS CYCLE

The word, the word
The cycle, lay, lay, lay
It's love cycles
God's love cycles

Cycles great, great shaking
The cycle is change
Cycle, cycle, God's tent, cycle
Cycle, now the cycle

Leaven, leaven: you're to shake
Leaven, leaven: you're to shake
Leaven – get, get this out
It's great shaking, great shaking

A shaking in the nations
A shaking in change
A great shaking you will see
A great love-seed

Love opens, opens, opens
Love cycle, love cycle
Love connects and love shakes
The cycle, the cycle, the cycle

The shaking: oh love, love, love
A shaking in your church
A great seed, a great seed
A great seed in hiding

The cycle, oh a great cycle
The cycle, oh what a change
A cycle of blending nations
A cycle of connecting nations

A cycle: more God, more love, more go
God loves, yes love
It's love for you, love for these
Love, love, yes love

God's love, love in this cycle
Oh leap, oh leap, oh leap
It's a cycle of change
A cycle of blessing, a cycle of abundance

Rituals, rituals, no, no, no
God, God, God stirs up
Love cycle, God-changing
It's great, it's seed, it's seed

Curtain, the curtain opens now, the curtain
Oh great curtain shows, shows
The day, the days of change increase
It's shaking, it's shaking and turning

Drizzle, drizzle, change, change
Bringing blessings, blessings, open Heaven
It's love, God's love
It's the cycle of love

The cycle opens, blessings come
The new change, the new change
The cycle, it's a turn, a turn
The cycle you see

It's connecting, it's stirring, it's change
The seeker, the seeker, he comes to see
It's nations, nations coming to see
It's love, it's love for your nation, you see

The token, the token of love
You're to see it come
It's seed, it's seed, it's blessing
The cycle, the cycle, is now

OH FATHER, FATHERS…

The Ghost, it's time for grace
Love releases change in you
You love, for you learn
Love, oh love is for you

Oh rely on love and rely on grace
Rituals, rituals, God's in change
Father, fathers: now you're to be, father
It's visiting, it's loving, it's growing

Gather seed gather love, gather, release
Rich, rich, bless, grow
Rebel, rebel: no, no, no
God is now opening, now
Bring and bring and love; heal, heal
Father, fathers, now bless and love

COUPLE'S LOVE & GRACE

Couple, couple, love and love
It's word, it's grace, it's my grace
And word! You are blessed
It's me in you

The word, the blessing, the blessing
It's word, it's love, it's grace
Do and do and do
And word is now, and word is do

The blessing, the blessing to do: change
Accuracy grace, accuracy grace
The accuracy, the accuracy
And God and grace

RISE, MARRIAGE, RISE

Marriages, miracles, Heaven
Shut, love and be
Shut and show the Father's light
Shut and love nations, shut in

Release and love and release
Show light and love and you
Wrestle, love, counsel love
Love sends light

Release God you see
Wrestle, go be love
Show love, love shoes
God and you and thee

Rise, love, be the word
Rise, love, be the Father's light
Rain, light, love Heaven
Rise, be the Father's light

So burn and light is love
Gale, gales, love, love be
Coach love, light God
Rise miracles and love the nation

Miracle counsels, light, love
Right, right, love be
So marriage, so gate, so Heaven
Go, love hands, rain be

Shut in, love and love
Send the hand and gate of Heaven
Relent and turn and love
Rise marriage, rise

Receive, dance, dance and be
Commit, commit, the word is nation
You see, you do, you are
God, light be, you see

LOVE DIRECTIVE

Shut your house
Shut your words
Love, love and love
You be, you bless, love
Darts, love, darts, bless
Enter, enter, abide and bless
Embers of blessing, open the blessing
Super open, super abiding
Secret enter, love and love
Yet I love and love, yes
Open love, God's here
Shut in, love God

Ballot, bless and bless
Love and love
Love blesses your marriage
You love, you live and bless
God lives and loves you: bless
Will yes, will light
Oh love you see, blend
Say and love the house

God's love burn love
Abundant and love and love
Let, let love abide
Let love open, love
Love – oh lead, oh lead
You are to live, love
Stay in love's hold
Yet it's God in you, see?

Stay and live in God
It's love, it's here – purpose
Oh love, love, boastings in love
God's light you are
This now, this love burns
God is love – forget!
Get, live, love
The Father loves your house
Submission, mission, love word
God will live in thee
The love, the love, forget, love
And burn with God, you see?

KISS, KISS, KISS, KISS

Lower and
      lower and
            lower,
                  Oh go
            and go
      and go
It's to hear my words
        It's to hear my love
                Oh God is blessing
                        He's abiding, he's doing
                There's a lesson in being
        And God is doing and doing
You are learning to be
        Open and open
                Oh daughter, son
                        God loves, loves, loves
                The waste is love
        Oh, but it's love
It's oh
        It's oh
            Oh!
                Oh!

WORDS OF LOVE TOO

♥ ♥

SECTION SEVEN

GOD'S BLESSINGS & GRACE

THE BLESSING IS COMING

Shine, shine, shine
The blessing is stirring on you
The blessing is being on you
The blessing is showing this day
And the blessing is opening things today

The blessing is on the place
The blessing is in your house
The blessing is bread, bread and bread
Keep in the blessing

The blessing is changing in you
The blessing is blowing in your house
The blessing is a teacher
Oh receive it! Receive it!

THE BLESSINGS ARE GOING

The blessings are going in this
The blessings are opening things
It's the blessing that turns things
The blessings are going

The blessings are coming
Love, love, oh receive
Love receives the blessing
Love works in the blessing

Love blesses and receives
Love loves to do
God is abundant love
The blessing is going but comes

It comes now more, more
Love is a blessing, love is to be
Oh blessing, oh blessing you're to have
Blessed, blessed, blessed
Blessed do receive, do have, do love

THE BLESSING OF BLESSING

The blessing of blessing
It's a thing to do
Daughters, sons are to receive
The blessing is now to be

God turns to share and share
The blessing: oh, oh, oh great things!
The blessing: oh, oh, oh what things!
Oh things of words
Oh great, great, great abundance

The blessing changes your church
The blessing will shake a church
The blessing is great and blowing in

The blessing is now in change
The blessing is an amazing thing
The blessing is bringing and doing
The hand, the hand, the hand

The hand on the house
The great blessing from me to thee
Shaking…learning to see
God loves blessing

THE BLESSING OF THE MITE

The blessing is on the mite
It is a sitting, it is a sitting
The blessing is on the mite that you sow

The blessing is on the mite
God is on this thing
The blessings are on this thing

The parting of this thing
It's super abundance as you sow
Come, come, sow the mite

Blessings are on it

THE BLESSING

It's love, it's God
It's God, it's love
The blessing...yes, yes, yes
It's you...yes, yes, yes

Love, God loves you
You are loved and loved and great
And loved and blessed and blessed
The blessed you are, the blessed you are

Release love and blessing
Love and blessing
It's blessing, it's love
It's God, it's you

Willing, willing, willing, it's love
Willing, willing, it's love and love
Bless you, love and love
And love and you and love and yes

Rolling, love, rolling love
It's love, it's God, it's your heart — relent
You're to bless, change and grow — relent
You're loving, you're sowing, you're seeing

Relent, love comes to see things
Love releases love and blessing
Relent and bless and love
God's love releases grace and blessing

Release love, release love
Bless, bless and love
Up, up, God comes to see love release
Love sees: it's love, it's love, it's blessing

BLESSED, BLESSED, BLESSED

Blessed, blessed, blessed
Blessing, blessing, blessing
Herod, Herod is not
Oh turn, turn and turn
The ache, the achings

Daddy loves love
Love is a blessing
Oh the blessing is in me
The blessing, blessing
Stirring, stirring and stirring

Delight, delighting
Oh character grace
Open, open, God is
He loves
Holy, holy is the one

Oh love, love and love
Love is a blessing
It's a blessing

THE BLESSING WAY

Way, way, way
The way is the word
The way is the blessing
The way is abundance

The way is to be
And the way is in me
The way is in change
And the way is abundant

Written, written
It's in me
The word is the key
It's the blessing, the blessing

The blessing, oh great it is!
The blessing you're to receive
Oh the blessing is in my purpose
It's in me

TO BE BLESSED

To be blessed, blessed, blessed
Oh blessed you are
Oh blessed in me, blessed in grace
God learning, God turning

Go blessing, go receive
You're blessed, you're blessed, you're blessed
Love blesses, love abides
Oh blessing, blessing: opening, opening
God learnt, God blessed

Yes loved, blessed, loved, blessed
Word, word, word
God learnt, learnt!
Guard it, guard it, guard and receive!

The word is blessing, the word is a blessing
God's secrets, God's blessings
Yes, oh yes! Open and receive
The past is now the past
Get, get and receive

Prayer: it's a grace to receive
The preach is amazed, it's amazed he is
He says not, not, not
God, not, not, not

He says not this, not that
God says, it's me, it's me, it's me
Chapel, chapel, chapel
God is open, open, open

God is abundant, God is love
Oh key – the key
God is in the blessing, God is in the word
The breaking, breaking, breaking
God's blessing is abundant blessing

THE SEER SHARES

The seer sees and releases
The seer releases love
The seer loves my love
The seer is grace and blessing

The seer is love, blessing, love
And the seer loves me
It's love, the seer loves nations
The seer is loving…the seer sees

The seer is love, is blessing
The seer releases love
The word, the word, the word
The seer loves my love

It's love in change
It's love in love
The seer is changing change
He is the love: he is love

YOU'RE TO BE

God opens you
You are to see
God is, he is
Yes and yes and yes

Oh, you are to be
You are to know
You are to see
You are to know

You are to stir
Separate, separate you are
You are open
You are abundant

It is, it is you are
You are open, you are to be
God is, he is!
Ha-Ha! Ha-Ha! He is!

Guiding and guiding and being
Adding and adding and doing
God opens and God opens
You are and you be

Hey, hey, hey, you are
You are – God is
It is, God is
You are open, you are to receive

Hype, hype, hype?
God is
God opens you to be
God and God he is

Boast in this and boast in this
God he is…he is
You to receive
You are to be

Barren, you are blessed
You are loved
You are abundant
Ho, ho and ho he is and he is

God's abundant
Oh it is, it is
God opens you to be
Oh go and do and be

It's go and go and do
And God will be
God says turn and be
It's to be, you're to be

Ho and do
Ho and go
Oh learn to do
Learn to see

Gold is in this
And gold is in this
And gold is in this
God is in this

Go and be and be and be
Diamond, diamond, diamond
Bread, bread, bread
Word and be: ha, ha, and ha!

God is going and doing and being
God grace, God blessing
Turn and receive and be
It's God and God and me

It's going and going and going
Gentle grace, gentle blessing
Gender is in God: ho and ho and ho
It is open to do, it is open to be!

Ho! God is – ho! He is
God and God it is
It's abundant; it's great
God answers you and God turns it

Guts, it's going to be guts
Stand and be and be
God is being
He is, he is

THE PICTURE

The picture is coming
God is going to open a thing
It's a picture of my love
God is love
Oh the picture is me
It's love, it's love, it's love
God and God loves, he loves
The will is me; the will is blessing
The picture is opening and opening
Oh the picture
What is it you say?
Oh the picture is grace, blessing, grace
There's a grace in the picture
It's telling grace, it's telling grace
The destiny of a church
The destiny of a nation
God and God
He's in the picture
Rich, rich, the picture is
Who you are is in the picture
Go and receive the picture

YOU'RE TO BE TOO

You're to be, you're to be
You're to be and you receive
The blessing is to be
Oh receive and be

THE MANY

This is a word, this is blessing
The word, the blessing, the blessing
Fear? No, no, no!
The mantle, the blessing, today is now
The many change, the many receive
The blessing on this, this and this
The blessing, the blessing you're released to do
Visitation, turning: blessing many

The mantle, the mantle, greater, great
The blessing is working on nations today
Rich, rich, leap up, grow, bless
It's now, it's now, forget and release

The many...there's doors for you
Daddy, the daddy loves you to grow and be
Door, door, love you!
The blessing, the blessing: forget and do
There are many, many nations
There are many things to do
The many things to release and be
God is on this nation

The man is now open today
Release, you're to do and be
God and God releasing nation
The many, the blessing

The door, the door
Things, words, change, love
God is now on nations
The many, the many you're to know and be
Leaven, leaven, it's time to change
Release and turn for many are coming
The word, the money, the blessing
The mantle, the door

God is on your church
Forget and do and do
The money...what you say?
Where, where? God is changing things

The day of grace is on your many
The mantle, the blessing, the day
God says be, love and do
The day of love is day
The blending, the blending, the door
The blessing is on thee and you
This is the day for you to turn
The door for you to go for God

The burn, the burn
It's time to be
For God is on many...and you!
It's going, it's doing, it's doing

The man: God's love you're to be
Things waking, waking, waking
The man, the house
Yet, yet, God's love
Things, kings, learn to be
The blessing, the love, the change
Hiding, hiding — but in grace
God sends nations to thee

God is on nations, nations
God is on change and change
Hide, hide, for God's love blesses you
These are blessings and love...forget

Things work as you worship
Ho-ho, ha-ha, yes!
The word, the blessing, the turn
Change and release things today
The God of blessings in on nations
And blessing, abiding, abundance
The blessing: God's love, God's love
Kings and change and bringing

It's word, it's word, it's change
Backing, the backing is changing and change
It's love, it's love, it's release and love
God loves to turn your heart and change

THE MANY (continued)

Things, waitings, waitings, waiting
God is opening the change
The blessing, the blessing is on your heart
God's love is on many, God's love is on many
The decent change, the decent love
Things will open and release
God is open...forget, forget
And God's working...forget, forget

Things opening
Blessing, blessing
Blending nations
A blending of nations

Couples, couples blessing nations
Releasing things, releasing love
God is now on change and change
The blessing, the blessing is on nations
It's time, it's time
Call, call and worship
And God is knowing
Change, but love is word!

IT'S GOD'S LOVE YOU SEE

The words of God, the words of light
The Father's kind light
The Father, signs of God
He is God and love is God

The love, the gate of God
Love is God's light
Heaven love times now
Heaven's love is now to be

Blendings, blessings, enter the beat
The Father, the blessings of love
It's love, it's God, it's now
Fathers, dads connect

This now, this enter, this day
Lesson, lesson, gates of love
Light, God's love for you
The Father, the blessing you be

The Father, the blessing to be
Heaven's love to see
Love, visitations, grace
Love, times, God's light

This love, this day yet is now
Wonders, visitations and love
Wonders and change you're seeing
You're soaking in love, in love

The Father's love is connecting love
You bless, you love, you sow
It's love, it's God's love visit
Enter the love of Heaven's love

The Father's gate now is
The blessing of God you are
Love connects you to God
Enter the door of love

The blessing, the Father you be
Wonder, wonders, signs and love
Light be, God's light see
Wonders and miracles see

It's Father's love, it's God's light
Open house, open house, miracles now see
Love and blessings enter your house
Oh love, oh Heaven, gate now see

The visit of love
Love you be, you see
The love, the love to see
Holy love see

It's time to be
Heaven's love to them
Love, love, mystery love
It's love, it's Heaven's love

The Father, let be
He is love, you be
You say, you live love
It's love, enter news of God

It's time you send love
Love gate enters now
Heaven's love, you are a blend
Mission, enter the Father

Love visit, love visit
Love is a visit in love
It's Heaven's love you be
Love, God's gate, see?

FASTING GRACE

Fasting grace, fasting love
Order: heart, heart, heart
Seal, seals, release and send
Command...and see my grace

Regenerate, love and love
A release, a release working grace, love
Seers blessing, seers going, doing

The least love, the least love
Soakers, love soakers
Seal, seal, release
The master abides...forget and release

Heal, heal, sow love, love
The master receives: love, and be!
The wrestle, the blessing, the might
The blessing, the blessing must abide

THERE'S BLESSING GRACE

There's blessings, oh grace
Oh blessing, but grace
Blessing in blessing in blessing
Love works, love work

Love is a key to grace
Love is a key to shaking
Oh grace, grace, blessing grace
Oh love is a thing, it's a thing of blessing

The blessing today is a grace to see
Lo, the thing is to see
Doors and blessings doors and blessings
A station is in you, a station is in me

Words, words, they sow blessing
Oh the word is the key to increase
The word is the key to abundance
Way, way, God is way
He is way, way, abundant
Oh blessing...oh love he is!

IT'S TIME TO SEE

See, see blessing
Oh love, see God
Oh see love, bless
See blessing, see grace

God loves grace
God loves signs
Holy miracles see
Holy miracles see

See love be
Holy miracle love
Holy mission see
See and see deep

Light, love, grace
Grace, grace, see
See love, see
Holy sign see

Grace, grace see
Words, grace see
Deep grace, deep grace
See love turn

Grace, grace, be
Holy time see
Grace shakes love
Holy day see

It's love, blessings, grace
Grace hears love
Love blend, grace
Yes, grace is love

HONOR GOD, SEE?

Go, God, go say
See my heart, see grace
Holy purpose, holy sign
See, burn. . .love

Purpose, vision, vision
Holy time be
See grace, you be
See, see, grace, see

Tents, love, God
Honor God's grace – love
Oh love, oh live, oh see
Say God's love, nation

Say, do, be light
Holy burn, holy time
Time of love you be
Sign, grace be

Sand, land bless
See God, live
See love, mercy
And see love, love

Prince, grace, cycle
See new grace now
Tears, love, prophesy
Honor God, see?

GOD'S SHAKINGS & SHAKINGS

God's shakings and shakings
Levee, levee, levee
It's open, open, open
Discern and discern and release

The ruling is abundant
Head, head and head
Learn, go and go
Whistlings: whistle, whistle

Love abundant, love hard
It's going, it's abiding, it's loving
Love: the word is to be
Ho, ho, ho! Bless, bless and bless

Released to go, released to go
The seal, the seal opens, open
The ballot but blessing
The ballot is blessed

Religion: not, not, not
God loves, God loves, God loves
God destined, it's God's grace
Jeer, jeer, jeer they do

But blessed is this, blessed is this
The gates of blessing open up
True, the blessings come – it's true, it's true
Releasing, releasing abundant power

Rubies, blessings, blessings
Gems of grace and gems of power
Rubies, God is opening rubies
There's jeering but blessing

Riddles, riddles, riddles
You're blessed, you're blessed, you're blessed
The shove, the shove – you're going in
God sends this and sends this

Rulings: they rule but I turn it
Sell, sell, sell, but I turn
Bless, bless, and bless
Awaking, awaking, awaking this

Tense, tense, tense – oh but it's tense
Loving love, I love, love, love
Ritual, they say the ritual
God is love, God is love

The amazed, the amazed – ha-ha!
God does and does this
It's a deal, it's a deal and it's a deal
It's time for this to come

VESSELS

God must abide in the vessel
The vessel is blending and doing
See, see, the word and the word
God's vessel, God's vessel

The vessel, the vessel, the vessel
Oh God is on the house
The vessel, God's love is on this
The vessel is on my heart

Visitations on vessels of grace
The visitation is on vessels of change
Oh visitation grace, visitation, vessel
Rich, rich grace

Forget and love and bless and bless
For God is growing vessels, vessels, vessels
The word, the vessel, the word
God is holding vessels

Here, there, where, there
God's love is on visitation love
Vessel, vessel, vessels, you are loved
For God is going to do this

It's God's vessel, it's God's love
The fight, the fight, but loved, loved
This and that
Releasing visitation

WORDS OF LOVE TOO

♥ ♥

SECTION EIGHT

HOLY AND ABIDING LOVE

IT'S OPEN, IT'S HOLY, IT'S HEAVEN

Hear, watch love
It's open, it's holy, it's Heaven
The gate, the gate opens, enter now
The Heaven, the gate, directions

This open door opens now
Holy and abiding is Heaven
The gate, the gate is Heaven
It's Heaven's day, yes, now is

This holy house, this Heaven
The God of gods loves and does
Holy love, holy day
The watch, the Heaven, love is light

The word, the gate, open Heaven
The Father, the Father, holy, he is
This holy house is holy
This holy day, yes

The Father does know hearts
Abide and love and see
Shaking change, shaking nation
The watch, the word, you see

A burn of Heaven see
It's watch, it's words, it's Heaven
Holy day, holy Heaven
The Father, the door, the gate

It's watching nation, day, light
It's holy God, light and love
This watch is holy
This word: Father and Heaven

It's holy time
This watch, this house
It's word, the Word
This watch is urgent

THIS TIME

This time, it's Heaven
This time, it's love
It's love-time
Holy it is

Time be
Yet be
It's time be
It's be love

This day, daytime
This time be
Holy day be
It's Heaven, it's God

This wind, this mercy
This wind of Heaven
This wind oh be
Holy is this wind

You see his wind?
You see this grace?
It's Heaven, it's God, it's you
It's love, it's you

IT'S HOLY

Seek, rise and love
See the love here
Holy things are now
Open the Father's light

Hands, souls, blessings
New season, living words
Healing miracles, miracles of love
Much God, yes

So holy you see
Open secrets, open doors
Holy vision dream
Healing, the word, the cycle

ABIDING DAY

Show the will of Heaven
Word and love
So abide in love now
So abide now

Holy and love be
Love be holy
Word of Heaven's Heaven
Love, abiding love

Holy day, holy time
Holy day, Heaven's see
Word and love in thee
See the Father's love

Holy day, abiding time
Abiding day in you
Abiding day in you
So open this now

HOLY DAY OF HEAVEN

Ten, sign, ten
Ten sign is
Sending days of gates shaking
Light be — say, say

So holy day
Receive and see
Worship, abiding light
Show, sow love

Worship, love-sign
Worship, mysteries of love
Wrestle, love and be
It's love in you to see

Holy day of God
Abiding love you see
Holy day of love is light
Holy day of Heaven

HEAVEN'S TIME

God is light
Enter his Heaven
Abide, love see light
Abide in the Heaven of light

Sendings, Heaven, send love
Holy time love now
Send holy, send holy
It's Heaven, it's Heaven send

Abide in love and Heaven
Holy day, love send
Holy day of Heaven now
See, see secrets of God

Open door, Heaven door
It's Heaven, it's Heaven door
Receive and love, his secrets
Sendings and turning now send

Commotion, love and live
Open door go now
Sendings and turnings of Heaven
Urgent – now turn, love

Show, show Heaven's love now
It's Heaven now, love
Open Heaven, do love
Open Heaven's love

Yes, live, live time
Send love now send
Receive and love and know
Abide, love and know

Purpose, Heaven, new days
Holy day see
See and know the Father
Commotion of God

Commotion now abide
Holy house, send love
It's Heaven day, say and say
It's Heaven house see

THIS GOD, THIS HEAVEN

It's love
It's Heaven
This living Heaven
This God is God

This love
He is Heaven
This living Heaven
This Heaven, is God

Oh holy abiding
This living Heaven
This loving Heaven
This Heaven, this Heaven

This God, is Heaven
The winds, the Father
This abiding Heaven
This God is God

HE AND HE IS

He and he is
Turning up
Abundant love
It's Heaven's, God's holy love

It's Heaven's abiding love
The Father is abiding
The will, the love he is
This God of love is
He and he is

LOVE OF LIGHT

Your sea, your sea
Your sea of love
Love in the house it is
Holy living in love

Oh, love
Oh live in the love
Holy is the day in light
It's time for nation to be

See the words of light
Light of love, miracle love
Love of love
Surging, light be

Holy is the man of God of love
His love is love
Love is in the house, it's in the house
So abide in the house

Oh rise, oh live in light
Holy is the love of Heaven
So abide in the Father
Holy is him

See the words and see his light
His love for thee you see
Holy is the love of Heaven
Receiving this nation

Soaking, dew of love
Holy burn, holy time
Show holy day of love
Sow time in love

See, be, here
Holy is this nation
Show living light
Love holy, now

Secret, light, holy now
Holy day of Heaven's light
Holy burning of Heaven
Holy, holy, yes

SEE AND SEE THIS

Shudders, shudders – God's holy
Light, light, God
This love of God
This holy God

The will, the will of love
This abiding love
This abiding Heaven
The love of Heaven

This holy Heaven
The loving God
The living God
This abiding here

This word, this time, this love
The will of Heaven's light
More God of light
The living Heaven

The will of love
This abiding God
This living gate
See and see it

RENDING AND SENDING

Rending and sending
Love busts and love abides
So holy, this holy gate
Love deep in love

This word, this Heaven, this Heaven
Love, God's door
This holy Heaven of God
This love, holy love

So love God
So holy deep in love
Loving and being in love
This abiding Heaven

This will, this holy deep
Time to love this and this
Loving and being in love
This holy sign is

This will, this will, this will
This love is God
So love and live
This holy deep God

Time, love, time
Love and live and say
Say his word and say
Say the word and say

Say the love and say the love
It's love and God and love
The Father is holy
It's love and God

LOVE MIGHT

Show might and love
Love might
Love, might, live!
See the Father's light

Abide and bless
Abide and live
Here and visitation, there
Holy day see

Receive and love
See his love
Holy day, holy time
Holy, holy here, now

See mercy in him
Holy is the Father
So holy his love is
So holy, the Father

The Father abides and does
Abide in him now
Holy is the love, he is
So here and there it is

Descending, descend
The Father's here
So abide in the day of love
Holy is the Father, holy

See his time, see the Father here
Holy time, he is
Blessed and loved he is
Abide you in him

Submission is grace
Rise and live in him
Show and live in him
Holy is the love in him

The seer of love, he is
Receive and love
Vision, days light here
So abide in love

The Father's holy day
Holy day, you are in this
You are holy, it's now
See the Father's love

Discern, discern, the love of God
Rod, rod of love it is
Love burns in him
Love will open things

Yes! Rise and live
Holy is him
Here is him
It's him

THE LIVING LOVE

Healing abundant
The living love
This Heaven does abide
This Heaven you see

The angel, the love, the Father
Things of Heaven release
Love does abide, love
The love of the Father

Yes, yes, yes, you see
The words of Heaven's love
Here's light, love and God
Here's Heaven, deep in love

Connecting in Heaven
It is Heaven in God
The words of love of God
The word of Heaven, the Father

The will of God, of love
This God does love
This God does abide
He abides in love

TRUE DEEP	SO LIVE DEEP
Deep is	Time, nurse time
Live deep	So live in deep
Deep, deep, deep	So live in deep
Live deep	So live deep
So deep	The word is turning deep
Live deep, live	So live the word
Oh live in deep	Deep is visions and vision
Deep this day	Holy deep is, yes
See deep, deep	So live deep, live love
Holy deep in love	Open doors of Heaven
Holy burn, holy deep	This day is now
Holy deep now see	So love and live
One day deep	The word is direct
Deep in love	The love of love
Deep, deep, deep, holy deep	So live holy, love
See the secret in love	So love, it is
So holy the love	See love in love
Deep love for you	So live holy love
So abide deep	Holy time do
Deep in the Father	Holy day love
Secret...deep	So love and live
Holy is him	So love holy
The Father, the Father	So live holy
He loves deep	So love, yes
	See this, see light
	This day of holy love
	The love of God you are
	This love is love
	This sign, this sign is Heaven
	So holy love see
	Yes love loves, live
	This love is you

NEW TURN

Turn, new turn see
Word is love
The word, the burn
The Father's love

Secrets of love
The Father's abiding
Word time...
Word now...

God word
Holy here
See now
Holy see

So holy see
Holy day mission
Holy season love
Word, holy day

Word of, holy, holy
So holy so see
Word, word, succor
So abide in him

Secret be
Holy, holy see
Holy secret, holy secret
The word here see

The word, the word of love
Holy, abiding holy
Abiding word of love
Holy is, secret

Soak and love and love
Holy, holy, holy yes
Love loves here, you
You hold it

Mercy gate of Heaven
Holy, holy, holy you
Holy yes, holy you
So holy, see

Soaking, sowing, live
Holy honor and love
Love is open now
Love holy now

Secret burn
Holy see
So holy now
Holy now

Secret...the word
Word, urgent, you are
Holy, holy, holy you
You see love

Secret...nation
Holy upper Heaven
The Father, the Father, holy
Heaven's holy

See the Father's love
Holy, holy love
Love holy now
Holy love see

The secret is here
The burn, the love
So holy you are
Love now...

SEE AND BE

You see, live, see, does live
See, live, time, live in him
See, live and be

Surges, surges of love
Yes, holy day, live
Holy time is
Abide and be
Holy day see
Wonders of love, holy day
You are holy

Sow time, sow here
Sow love in love
So abide in love

You're to know his light
Heaven and here
Holy time here
Holy is the Father
Show love wholly
The light is entering the house

Receive and see
Time…is…yes
Yes, oh you see

Shudders of this nation
Holy is the light in thee
See healing in thee
Oh you know love
Soaking in love
Holy abiding in you

Abide, this nation
You see, in thee
Race, race, holy time
Yes, oh live in him
Holy mantle abiding now
See light in you
Surging love in thee

The Father's love in you
Shut into the Father's love
Yes, holy is the nation

SURGING

Destiny, mission, God
See the word of love
See his word in thee
You be the Father's light

Surging love of God
Surging Heaven, do for love
So abide in love you be
Light be, live and see

Secret – abiding light
Sign, sign, light, light be
Sign of light is now
Time, time be

See things in love
Surge, love, surge
Turn, turn now, live
Surge and surge in love

Surge, in love, in him
It's love of the Father
Surging God is entering the now
Oh sign in love in God

YET !!

Yet it is love
Oh what is love?
It's God, he is
Yet it's God

Love, watching love
It is time for love
Oh the day of God
Oh a time in God

Holy God, love and love
Yet love opens a house
Releasing and blessing
Yet abiding love

This time yes
Yes, it's time
Loving the nation
Loving and being

Yet it's day
Oh it's time
Oh love is now
Oh love is yes

Yes it's now the love
Oh love is yes
Why, why they say
Love works, love does

You are to know the love
It's God and love
Send love and send love
Love, oh now

It's the love that releases now
You are to live in the gate of love
God abides in grace
And grace and love

THE ABIDING NOW IS

You love and lo, love
It's time to increase love
Upper Heaven, upper Heaven
It's time to abide

A surrender to God is now
It's a sender of God
It's a sender of Heaven
Dear, dear, love God

The seer, the seed, the God
Upper Heaven: love is love for these
Ocean, loving nations
Upper Heaven: mercy, love, nation

You're to sow love and love
Upper Heaven, mystery of Heaven
Release now love and God
Upper Heaven, great nations, increase grace

Succeed…love these
Mission of Heaven to go
Angels coming to see
It's love you have for this and these

The rock of God
The love of Heaven
It's love for him
It's love for you

You're to love, you're to sow, you're to know
Release and love and sow
Release the here and there
And love and abide and know

Upper Heaven and sow love and sow love
It's love, it's you, it's God
Upper Heaven: love is for thee
It's love, it's you, it's these

Release and lead and go

Share your thoughts

Feel free to judge this work by way of the Holy Scriptures and prayer. And if you would like to share how this collection of poetry has blessed you, as well as any prayer requests you may have please write to me at:

PO Box 441648
Indianapolis, Indiana 46244
United States of America

theseer1959.wordpress.com

twitter.com/theseer1959